Contents

63
Discover emojis and accents

69
Choose a new wallpaper

41
Talk to Siri

MacBook

For
Seniors

Welcome

The MacBook is one of the most useful pieces of technology you can buy. Once you're comfortable using the trackpad to open apps, you'll soon be able to browse the internet, send messages, make video calls, and even explore the world from above.

The best thing about the MacBook, however, is that it's so easy to use, and if you're ever unsure what to do, then you can simply ask Siri -- the Mac's digital assistant.

This book is all about making sense of the MacBook, even if you've never used one before. You'll learn about the very basics, how the built-in apps work, and how you can use a MacBook to enrich and improve your life. Large images and step-by-step guides are used throughout to help you along the way. Turn over the page and you'll find the book contents, which provides a brief glance at what you can expect to find in each chapter. Alternatively, jump to the back of the book to see a more detailed index.

As you become more familiar with the MacBook and its apps, you might have specific questions that aren't covered in this book. If so, feel free to send me an email at tom@leafpublishing.co.uk, and I'll be more than happy to help.

Tom Rudderham
Author
tom@leafpublishing.co.uk

Credits:

Author: Tom Rudderham
Editor: Zeljko Jurancevic
Copy Editor: Kaye Inglis

Published by:
Leaf Publishing LTD
www.leafpublishing.co.uk

ISBN:
9798675862122

109
Learn how to edit your photos

125
Explore the world in 3D

153
Extend the battery

Terminology

Wondering what all those words and phrases mean?

The MacBook is a state of the art piece of equipment, so perhaps it's inevitable that talking about it involves using a wide-ranging assortment of words, phrases, and terminology. In this book, you're going to hear a lot about the MacBook hardware, software, and features. Don't worry, each one of them will be explained as we go, so you'll never feel confused or get lost halfway through a paragraph. To get you started, here are a few of the words we will be using constantly throughout this book...

Hardware

Whenever the word hardware is used, we're basically talking about the MacBook in its physical form. The thing which sits on your lap.

Software

Think of software as a set of instructions for doing something on your MacBook. These instructions might be millions of words long, and they were probably written by a large team of people. To most humans, it's utter gibberish. It looks something like this:

```
int main(int argc, char * argv[]) {
    @autoreleasepool {
        return UIApplicationMain( argc, argv, nil,
NSStringFromClass( [AVCamAppDelegate
class] ) );
    }
```

To a programmer who writes in Swift (Apple's programming language), this makes perfect sense. It's just a fraction of the code required to tell your MacBook how to capture an image using its camera. The full piece of code is tens of thousands of lines long.

App

The word app is short for application. An application is a piece of software, separate from macOS, which lets you do something. There's an app on your MacBook for browsing the web. There's an app for sending messages. There's an app for looking at your photos. I'm sure you get the idea.

macOS

This is the name of the software which powers your MacBook. It's one of the most complicated pieces of software ever created by man. It tells your Mac how to turn on, how to take a photo, how to browse the internet, how to scan your fingerprint when you want to unlock your Mac plus so much more. It can also learn over time. macOS will learn about your habits, how you type to individual people, where you travel, and what you sound like. It uses all of this learning to help you type quicker, find photos quicker, and basically use your Mac in a more efficient manner.

You don't have to worry about security either, because all of this personal information is fully encrypted, and the really important stuff, like your fingerprint, never leaves your Mac.

When most people think of the word macOS, they imagine the desktop on their Mac. You can think of it like that too, but really it's so much more.

Third-party apps

These are apps created by companies other than Apple. There are tens of thousands of them, and each app serves its own purpose. For example, using Photoshop you can edit photos professionally, while an app like Sketch enables you to design mobile apps. You'll find all of these apps in the...

App Store

Think of the App Store as a market for apps. Some apps are free, others cost a few dollars/pounds/euros. Some apps look like they are free, but ask for a payment to do something (this is called an "In-App Purchase"). You can find the App Store on your MacBook. It has a bright blue icon with an abstract "A" in the middle.

Encryption

Think of encryption as a padlock for words, but instead of 0-9 on the padlock, it's A-Z, plus 0-9. The software on your Mac uses encryption all the time. Whenever you send a message to a friend, all the letters you type are scrambled up, sent to the other person, then de-scrambled on their device. The same goes for video calls you make using FaceTime, your credit card's details when you check out on the internet, and much more. Nearly everything you do on your Mac is encrypted.

iCloud

Think of iCloud as a computer somewhere in the world where your photos, messages, apps, and settings are stored. Your Mac talks to this computer over the internet every day to backup new photos, send new messages, and check for updates.

Terminology continued

Browser

This is the term used to describe an app for navigating the internet. On the Mac, the "browser "is called Safari, but there are other browsers available to install from the App Store, such as Chrome, Firefox, and Microsoft Edge.

Restart

The word "restart" is used when something needs to be turned off, then back on again. Maybe your Mac needs to be restarted because it has stopped working, or similarly an app might need to be restarted.

Siri

Think of Siri as a virtual assistant that you can talk to. You can ask Siri what the weather is like, directions to somewhere, basic math questions, or even the answers to trivia.

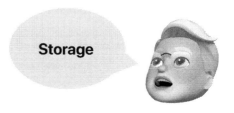

Storage

Your Mac comes with a limited amount of space for storing photos, videos, apps, and other content. When you bought your Mac, you needed to choose how much storage it had available, and the more storage space you chose, the more expensive it was to buy.

Sleep

You can put your MacBook to sleep by closing the lid. When it's asleep, it will still check for new messages, emails, and notifications, but it won't use much power. In sleep mode, your Mac can last for nearly a week on a full battery charge, while in normal use (when the screen is on), it's somewhere inbetween 10 and 20 hours.

Gigabyte / GB

This storage comes in gigabytes (AKA GB), with the base MacBook Air and Pro coming with 256GB of storage, and the 16-inch MacBook Pro with 512GB.

To put that into context, you can typically save around 250 photos per gigabyte, or approximately 10 minutes of video.

Settings

You can heavily configure how your MacBook notifies you of new messages, how bright the screen is, how loud the speakers are, and even how apps track your location. These configurations are called "settings', and to make any of these changes (plus much more), then you need to open the System Preferences app.

Gestures

When we talk about gestures on the MacBook, we're referring to the use of your fingers to initiate an action on the trackpad below the keyboard. Let's say you want to zoom into a photo. The gesture to do this would be to place two fingers on the trackpad then move them apart.

Desktop

The Desktop is the first place you see after unlocking your Mac. Most of the time it's just a wallpaper image, with the Dock at the bottom of the screen, and the Apple Menu at the top, but you can add folders and files on the Desktop and then use it as a place to store things for quick access.

Attachments

If you receive an email that includes a photo, video, or document, then it is usually referred too as an attachment.

Don't understand another term?

Feel free to email Tom, the author of this book at tom@leafpublishing.co.uk, and he'll be happy to explain any further terms or phrases that you're unsure about.

Icon

The small image that represents an app is usually referred too as an "icon". It's basically a small image that when clicked on, let's you open an app, or initiate an action.

Things to keep in mind

The MacBook is easier to use than you might think...

Whether you've just bought your new MacBook, or been given one by a friend or family member, there are a few things to keep in mind.

You do nearly everything with the trackpad

That large rectangle below the keyboard is called the trackpad. It works by detecting the static from your fingertip, and enables you to move a small arrow around the screen. This arrow is called the cursor. To interact with anything on your Mac's screen, move the cursor over it then press down firmly on the trackpad to initiate an action. This action is called a click.

This is what the cursor looks like.

You can never do the wrong thing

You'll never break your MacBook by opening the wrong app, or by tapping on the wrong key, so don't worry about making a mistake. Most apps have sensible names, so if you want to send a message, open the Messages app, and if you want to look at photos, click on the Photos app.

If you're unsure about an app, feel free to open it anyway, you can always close it by moving the cursor to the top of the screen, clicking on the name of the app in the top-left corner, then **Quit**.

This is how Siri looks.

You can talk to your Mac

Your Mac has a built-in assistant called Siri (covered in more detail later in this book). You can use Siri to do basic things like making a FaceTime call, perform simple maths, set a reminder, or set a timer. To do this, click the **Siri** icon in the top-right corner of the Apple Menu ( ), then say out-loud something like "remind me to take the dinner out of the oven in 10 minutes", or "what's 15 times 30?". After a moment or two, Siri will perform your request.

You don't need to buy any software for your Mac

Your Mac comes with all the apps and tools needed to safely browse the web, write documents, edit photos, and even create music. To give a couple of examples, if you need to visit a website, there's an app called Safari, and if you need to create a spreadsheet, then there's an app called Numbers. You don't need to install any antivirus software either, as Mac's are fully protected against threats on the web via regular software updates that are totally free.

Here are just a few of the apps included with your Mac.

The are two kinds of MacBook

Browse the Apple website, and you'll quickly notice there are two types of MacBook:

MacBook Air

A beautiful, light, and fast laptop. The MacBook Air is perfect for anyone planning to browse the web, enjoy media, and stay in touch with friends and family.

MacBook Pro

Available in two sizes: 14" or 16", the MacBook Pro is aimed at the more professional and creative type of person. It's powered by Apple's M1 Pro chip, one of the fastest and most efficience processors available.

Whichever MacBook you own, this book covers everything you need to know, including how to setup your Mac, use its apps, make video calls, plus much more.

MacBook Air: hardware

A brief look at the MacBook Air's main features...

1 Camera
Using this camera, you can make video calls or take a photo of yourself.

2 Display
The MacBook Air's pin-sharp display shows text and videos with vivid clarity.

3 Keyboard
The keyboard is fully backlit, ensuring you can continue to type in low-light or the dark. In the top-right corner is the Touch ID button, which enables you to use your fingerprint to confirm your identity or make purchases.

4 Microphone
Tucked away in the top-corner of the keyboard is a small microphone.

5 USB-C ports
Using these two ports, you can plug other devices into the MacBook Air, such as memory cards, iPhones, or even an external monitor. This is also where you insert the power cable.

6 Trackpad
Use this trackpad to move the cursor around the screen. You can also perform Multi-Touch gestures with your fingers.

MacBook Air: keyboard

A quick overview of the keyboard rows and shortcuts...

1 Brightness
Press **F1** to increase the brightness of the display, or **F2** to reduce it.

2 Mission Control
Press **F3** to open Mission Control, which enables you to quickly move between working spaces.

3 Launchpad
Press **F4** to quickly access all of the apps installed on your Mac.

4 Keyboard Brightness
Adjust the brightness of the keyboard backlight with **F5** and **F6**.

5 Audio playback
Press **F7** to rewind or jump to the previous item. Press **F8** to play and pause music. Press **F9** to fast-forward through audio or skip to the next item.

6 Volume Controls
Press **F10** to decrease the volume level, **F11** to increase it, and **F12** to mute the audio.

7 Power and Touch ID button
Press and hold this button to turn on your Mac. This button also acts as a fingerprint sensor, enabling you to confirm your identity and pay for items using Apple Pay.

8 Function Key
Some apps still support traditional function keys (**F1** - **F12**). Hold down this button then press a function key, and it will work like a standard function key, rather than a shortcut.

9 Modifier Keys
Press **Shift** to type capital letters or symbols. Press **Option** or **Command** to perform keyboard shortcuts.

MacBook Pro: hardware

A brief look at the MacBook Pro's main features...

① Camera

Using this 1080p camera, you can make video calls or take a photo of yourself.

② Display

The MacBook Pro's pin-sharp screen displays text and videos with vivid clarity. It's powered by mini-LED's, has a 120Hz refresh rate, and can display up to 1,000,000,000 colours.

③ Headphone socket

Plug a pair of traditional headphones into your Mac using this socket.

④ Keyboard

Set in a double-anodised black well, the latest MacBook Pro keyboard brings back the standard F keys, while still including support for Touch ID.

⑤ Magsafe & USB-C ports

The Magsafe port is a safe and powerful way to charge your MacBook. The two USB-C ports enable you to plug other devices into the MacBook Pro, such as memory cards, iPhones, or even an external monitor.

⑥ Trackpad

Use this trackpad to move the cursor around the screen. You can also perform Multi-Touch gestures with your fingers.

MacBook Pro: keyboard

A quick overview of the keyboard rows and shortcuts...

1 Brightness
Press **F1** to increase the brightness of the display, or **F2** to reduce it.

2 Mission Control
Press **F3** to open Mission Control, which enables you to quickly move between working spaces.

3 Launchpad
Press **F4** to quickly access all of the apps installed on your Mac.

4 Do Not Disturb
Press **F6** to instantly activate Do Not Disturb on your Mac, which disables notifications and FaceTime calls from coming through to your Mac.

5 Audio playback
Press **F7** to rewind or jump to the previous item. Press **F8** to play and pause music. Press **F9** to fast-forward through audio or skip to the next item.

6 Volume Controls
Press **F10** to decrease the volume level, **F11** to increase it, and **F12** to mute the audio.

7 Power and Touch ID button
Press and hold this button to turn on your Mac. This button also acts as a fingerprint sensor, enabling you to confirm your identity and pay for items using Apple Pay.

8 Function Key
Some apps still support traditional function keys (F1 - F12). Hold down this button then press a function key, and it will work like a standard function key, rather than a shortcut.

9 Modifier Keys
Press **Shift** to type capital letters or symbols. Press **Option** or **Command** to perform keyboard shortcuts.

The very basics

Get started with your MacBook...

Powering on and off

To turn on your MacBook, press and hold the **Power** button in the top-right corner of the keyboard.

To turn your MacBook off, click on the **Apple** logo in the top-left corner of the screen, then click **Shut Down...**

Sleep mode

Your Mac will automatically lock itself and go into sleep mode when you close the lid. When it's asleep, it will still check for new messages and emails, but the screen will be turned off, and it will use less power.

To wake your MacBook up, simply open the lid.

Adjust settings

To adjust a large number of settings, look for the app within the Dock which has a cogwheel in its centre. By opening this app, you can change the wallpaper, cursor speed, language, and much more. Jump to the System Preferences section towards the back of the book for more about settings.

Understand windows

Nearly everything you do on your Mac is through a window. Think of a window as a sheet of paper on a desk, and you'll begin to understand how it works. With this piece of paper, you can view an app, a document, or a collection of files. You can have as many pieces of paper on the screen at once, you can slide them around to organise them, and you can stack them on top of each other.

You can learn more about windows in the "Desktop" chapter.

Access Control Centre

Think of Control Centre as a place where you can change the screen brightness, adjust the volume, and access several other settings. You can access Control Centre by clicking the **Control Centre** button (⬒) in the top-right corner of the screen.

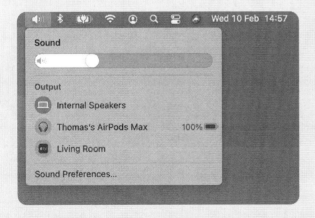

Adjust the volume

You can adjust the volume level in a number of ways:

- On a MacBook Air, press **F11** to turn the volume down, or **F12** to turn it up.
- On a MacBook Pro, use the volume buttons on the Touch Bar to make adjustments.
- You can also click on the audio button in the top-right corner to adjust the volume and connect to other devices, such as headphones.

The Login Screen

How to select a user and login...

If your Mac is turned off, hold down the **Power** button in the top-right corner of the keyboard, and after a moment it will power on. You'll then see the login screen:

An overview of the Login Screen:

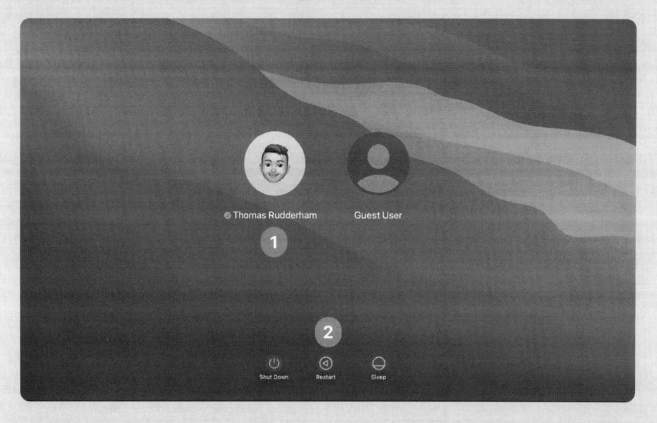

When you reach the Login Screen, you may see a number of users displays across the centre of the screen. Alternatively, if your Mac is set to log you in automatically, then you may bypass this screen entirely and go straight to the desktop (see number one across the page to set this up or disable it).

1 Click on your username using the trackpad or a mouse. The login window will then appear. Enter your password, then either click **Log In** or press the **Enter** key on the keyboard. If you have forgotten your password, click on the **Hint (?)** button, and your Mac will display a password hint.

2 These shortcuts at the bottom of the screen enable you to turn off your Mac, restart it, or put it to sleep. In sleep mode, your MacBook will remain on but barely use any power. This is helpful if you know that you're going to use your Mac again in the next day or two

Customise the Login Screen

You can customise the Login Screen in several ways. For example, it's possible to automatically skip the Login Screen, hide the password hint, and enable a number of accessibility options. To do this, open the **System Preferences** app (you'll find it in the Dock -- its icon looks like a set of cog wheels), click on **Users & Groups**, then click the **padlock** icon in the lower-left corner.

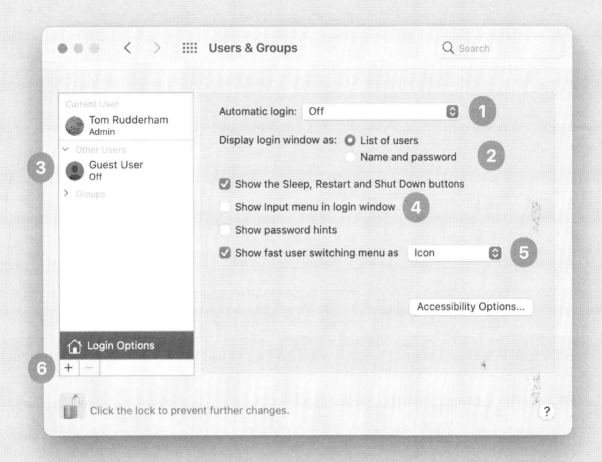

1. Automatic login will bypass the Login Screen entirely. This is helpful if you're the only one with access to your Mac.

2. With **List of users** selected, the Login Screen will display the names of each user on your Mac. When **Name and Password** is enabled, each user will have to manually enter their name and password.

3. If you're the admin user for your Mac, then you can select another user then change their password and login items (apps which automatically open when they log in).

4. Tick **Show Input menu in login window** to let users choose the language they see after login.

5. This lets you quickly switch between users from the Login Screen. The dropdown menu enables you to choose how user accounts are displayed.

6. To add a new user account, click the **plus** (+) button. To remove an account, select it in the sidebar above, then click the **minus** (-) button.

Touch ID

Unlock your MacBook using your fingerprint...

Touch ID is pretty amazing. It works by recognising your fingerprint when you place it on the small black square in the top-right corner of the keyboard. Once enabled, you can unlock your Mac with your fingerprint, or purchase an item over the internet using Apple Pay.

It's worth noting that your Mac and its operating system can never access your fingerprint record. Instead, it's stored in a secure part of the Touch Bar hardware; and it never leaves the Touch Bar, so when you place your fingerprint on the sensor, either a yes or no signal is sent to the operating system.

Keeping your personal data safe is one of Apple's most pressing priorities, so here's what the company does to ensure your fingerprint never leaves your MacBook:

- The MacBook and its operating system can never access your fingerprint. Instead, it's stored in a secure part of the Touch ID bar.

- Your fingerprint never leaves the physical device. That means it can't be accessed by the NSA, hackers or anyone else.

How to set up Touch ID

1 Your Mac will ask you to set up Touch ID when you activate it for the very first time. If you skipped that step, just click on the **Apple** menu button on the top-left of the screen, click **System Preferences**, select **Touch ID,** then click **Add a fingerprint**.

2 Place your thumb or finger on the Touch ID sensor. You'll see a graphic of a fingerprint appear and slowly start to turn red. Keep placing your fingerprint on the sensor until the graphic has completely turned red. The next step is to capture the surrounding areas of your fingerprint. This is to ensure the sensor can read your finger when it's tilted or leaning to one side. The most efficient way to complete this process is to place your finger on the sensor at an angle, lift it, roll your finger slightly then place it down again.

3 Repeat this process until you've rolled your finger all the way around and the graphic has turned red. Next, click the **Continue** button. Your fingerprint has been added and can now be used.

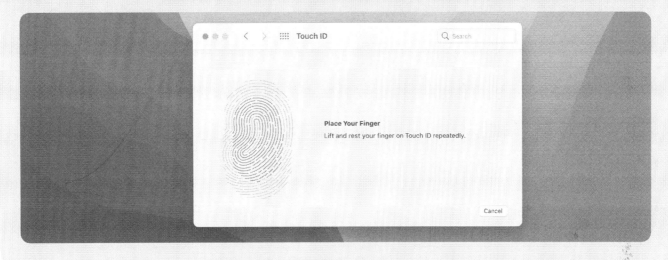

Fingerprint options

Now that you've added a fingerprint, you'll notice checkbox buttons which enable you to unlock your MacBook, purchase items using Apple Pay, and enter passwords. Tick any of the options you wish to use.

Delete a fingerprint

To remove a fingerprint, simply hover the cursor over the fingerprint, then click the small **X** button which appears. You can also name fingerprints by clicking on the finger name, then typing a replacement into the text field.

Connect to a Wi-Fi network

Easily connect to home, office, or public Wi-Fi networks...

Connecting to a Wi-Fi network is one of those really basic tasks that we all must do from time to time. Perhaps you're visiting a friend and would like to hook up to their internet connection, or you might be sat in a coffee shop that offers free Wi-Fi.

When you first activate your Mac, you'll be asked to connect to the nearest Wi-Fi network and walked through that process. If you skipped that step, or need a reminder, then here's how to connect to a Wi-Fi network on your Mac:

Connect to Wi-Fi

1. Begin by clicking on the **Wi-Fi** icon (📶) in the menu at the top of the screen.

2. A list of Wi-Fi connections will appear in the drop-down menu.

3. Select a wireless network. You might see a small padlock icon next to some of the networks, which means they require a password before you can join. If so, the password entry screen will appear, enabling you to enter a password and click **Join**. If you've entered it successfully, then your Mac will automatically join the network.

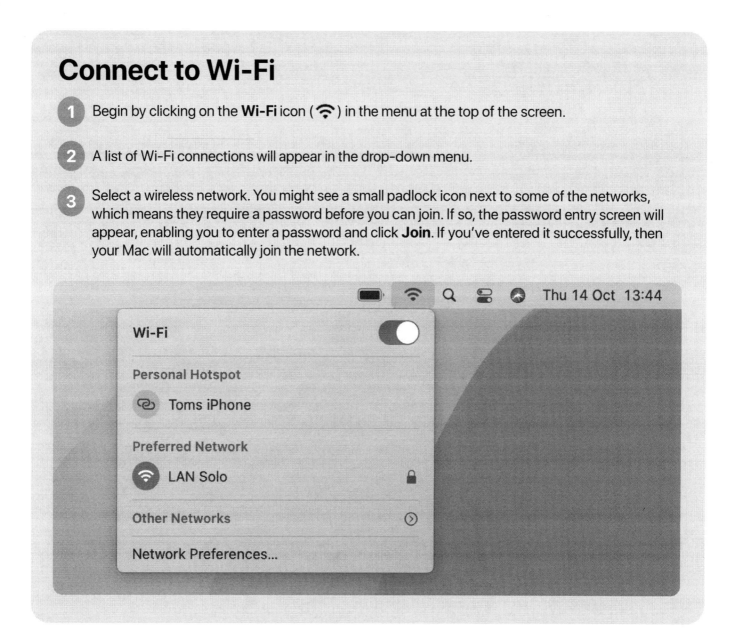

Configure a preferred Wi-Fi network

If you want to explore the Wi-Fi settings on your Mac or make some changes, then here's how it's done:

1. Open **System Preferences**, then click on **Network**.

2. Click the **Advanced** button in the lower-right corner.

3. You'll see a list of all the Wi-Fi connections you Mac has connected to, in order of preference. If there are two available locally, then your Mac will always connect to the one at the top.

4. If you want to change this order, simply **click and drag** the connections up and down.

5. To remove a network connection, click on it, then click the minus button below the list.

Public networks

If the network doesn't require a password then you can simply click on the Wi-Fi network name and immediately connect to the web. Note however, that sometimes networks require you to enter personal details via the Safari app before you can freely browse the web. You'll probably come across this situation in coffee shops and airports. Hotels might also request you to enter your hotel room number and a password, the latter of which is typically available from the reception.

Problems with WiFi

In case you encounter some issues with the Wi-Fi, here are a few things you can try to remedy it:

1. Make sure the router is switch on and is connected. You can usually do this by looking at the router. If it has green lights flashing, then everything is fine. If there seems to be a problem, try disconnecting the power, reconnecting it then wait a few minutes.

2. Check the Wi-Fi signal on your Mac. You'll see it in the menu bar in the upper right corner. If the signal is strong, then you'll see four bars. If you see less, try moving your Mac closer to the router. Thick walls can also block the connection.

Customise the Dock

Learn how to use and customise the Dock...

Think of the Dock as a shortcut to the Finder and all of your favorite applications, folders, and files. If you use something regularly, keep it in the Dock and it's never more than a click away.

When you first activate your Mac you'll see the Dock at the bottom of the screen, with the following items arranged from left to right:

- **The Finder**
- **Launchpad**
- **Default Apps**
- **System Preferences**

- **Currently-running apps**
- **Favorite files or folders**
- **The Trash**

The Dock is surprisingly flexible. You can resize it, rearrange items within it, snap it to the side of the screen, or even hide it when it's not needed. Here's how it looks on a brand new Mac:

Add an app to the Dock

If you regularly use an app then it's a good idea to add it to the Dock. Not only does that save time, but you'll also be able to see when the app is running on your Mac via a small dot underneath its icon.

To add an app from the Applications folder...

1. Open a Finder window, then click **Applications** in the sidebar.

2. Click and hold on an app, then drag it to the Dock.

3. Let go of the app while it's hovering over the Dock and it will drop into place.

If an app is already open on your Mac...

1. **Right-click** or **Control-click** on the app icon in the Dock.

2. Hover the cursor over **Options**.

3. Click on **Keep in Dock**.

Remove something from the Dock

If you want to remove something from the Dock, just click on the app, folder or file, then drag it off the Dock. You'll instantly see it disappear. You can also **right-click** or **Control-click** on the app icon, move the cursor over **Options**, and then un-select **Keep in Dock**.

Rearrange items in the Dock

Most users place their most recently used apps on the left, while others group them by type. However you want to organise your Dock, it's easy to move apps around; simply click and hold on an app icon, then move it to where you want it to go.

Choose how folder contents appear

Whenever you click on a folder in the Dock, your Mac reads its contents then displays them in a number of ways:

- If there are less than 15 items within the folder, you'll see a "Fan" arrangement appear, where the items are stacked one above the other.

- If there are 15 items or more within the folder, you'll see a fixed grid layout appear.

If you prefer one arrangement over the other, and want to set a default preference, **right-click** on the folder within the Dock, look for "**View content as**" in the pop-up window and choose your preference. You'll also see a third option called List, which displays the folder contents as a (you guessed it) list.

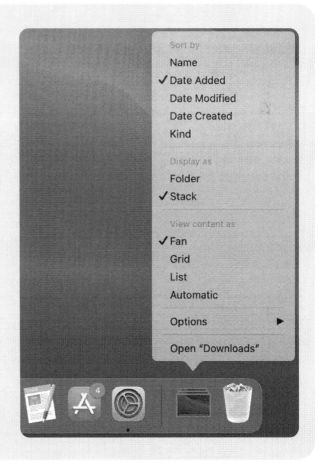

Make the Dock bigger or smaller

By default the Dock takes up a considerable amount of space at the bottom of the screen. By making it smaller not only do you gain more vertical space for apps and content, but you can also add more apps, folders, and shortcuts to the Dock. Here's how to adjust the size of the Dock to your liking:

A tiny Dock...

A large Dock...

1 Open the **System Preferences** app and click **Dock & Menu Bar**.

2 Drag the **Size** slider left or right to increase or decrease the size of the Dock. You'll see it change in real-time as you move the slider.

3 Alternatively, if you hover the mouse over the faint black line on the Dock which separates apps from folders and files, you'll see the cursor turn to a double-headed arrow. By clicking and dragging left or right, you can adjust the size of the Dock without going into System Preferences.

Make Dock items zoom as you scroll over them

The Dock has a great visual animation effect which 'zooms' icons into view as you move the cursor over them. Here's how to enable and tweak the effect:

1 Open the **System Preferences** app and click **Dock & Menu Bar**.

2 Tick the **Magnification** box, then drag the **Magnification** slider left or right to adjust the effect.

3 Test the effect by hovering the cursor over an app in the Dock.

Snap the Dock to the side of the screen

As you might have already noticed, your MacBook display is wider than it is tall. This is great for watching movies or browsing through photos, but can restrict your view when browsing web pages or writing long documents.

If you want to gain a little bit of extra vertical space, then snapping the Dock to the left or right side of the screen is a good idea. To do this:

1. Open the **System Preferences** app and click **Dock & Menu Bar**.

2. Look towards the middle of the next panel and you'll see options for placing the Dock on the **Left, Bottom** (default) or **Right**. Click on an option to see how it looks and feels.

Add spaces to the Dock

If you're a professional user, chances are you have a *lot* of apps, folders, and files in your Dock. To help organise your Dock, it's possible to add spaces between apps or folders to help you categorise them. It's a little fiddly and requires using the Terminal app, so this is only recommended for those who feel confident using their Mac. Here's how:

1. Open the **Terminal** app.

2. Enter the following text, as many times as you wish, to add spaces: **defaults write com.apple. dock persistent-apps -array-add '{"tile-type"="spacer-tile";}'**

3. Force restart the Dock to make the spaces appear by entering this into Terminal: **killall Dock**

You can move spaces around by clicking and dragging them, and you can remove them by dragging them off the Dock.

Add an email account

Learn how to add your email account, calendar, and contacts...

As you use your Mac to explore the internet, you'll soon realise how important an email account is. It's basically a virtual postbox, letting you send and recieve messages, and register for services on the web. On this page you'll learn the basics of adding an email account. Most of it happens automatically, and once you've added an account you'll be able to start emailing friends and family, check your calendar for events, plus much more.

Add your email account

1 Start by opening the **System Preferences** app, then click on **Internet Accounts**.

2 Select your email provider. If your email address ends with "gmail.com", then click on Google. If it ends with "hotmail.com", select the Microsoft Exchange option.

3 Your Mac will ask for the username and password associated with your email account. Simply enter these and click **Next**.

4 Some providers, such as Gmail, will require that you enter your details using Safari.

5 Your Mac will verify your mail account details. Once the process has completed you can choose whether you wish to sync mail, contacts and notes.

Add contacts, calendar entries, and notes

If you've ever used your Gmail or Outlook account to add contacts, calendar events, and notes, then your Mac can automatically load these from the internet and add them to your Mac. To do this:

1 Open the **System Preferences** app, then click on **Internet Accounts**.

2 Click on your account.

3 On the following screen, tick the **Contacts**, **Calendars**, and **Notes** options.

Add a custom email account

If you have a custom email account – perhaps associated with work or a personal website - then it's possible to enter its details and access your emails through the Mail app. Adding an account isn't as easy as simply entering a username and password, you'll also need the server details and choose whether to use IMAP or POP3 (explained shortly).

1 Start by opening the **System Preferences** app, then click on **Internet Accounts**.

2 Click **Add Other Account...** at the bottom of the list, then select **Mail account**.

3 In the Name field, enter the name you wish recipients to see when they receive your email. Next, enter your email address and password used to access your account.

4 Click **Sign In** and your Mac will attempt to verify the account. It will then ask you to choose an IMAP or POP account type. IMAP accounts store emails on the internet, enabling you to check your email account from multiple sources, such as your Mac or an iPhone. A POP account stores emails *only* on your Mac, meaning the account can only be accessed from that device.

5 For Incoming Mail Server, enter the server address for your email account. It might be something like imap.example.com. For the Outgoing Mail Server field, enter the outgoing server address. It's usually something like smtp.example.com. Click **Sign In**, and if everything is correct, your custom email account will be added to your Mac.

If you need help getting hold of your custom email account details, please contact your email provider. They will be able to give you the incoming and outgoing server details.

Add a printer

Set up a printer then print from your Mac...

Printing documents from your Mac is an essential task for anyone working from home. Maybe you need to print a letter to friends or family, or perhaps you'd like to sign, print, and send a document. Whatever the reason, you'll be glad to hear that it's easy to add a printer and get started.

Choosing a printer

If you don't have a printer yet, then here are some tips for finding the right one for you:

- Look for a printer that supports AirPrint. Your Mac will automatically recognise this type of printer, which makes it easier to set up, and avoids potential compatibility problems.

- If you're planning to print documents on a regular basis, consider getting a laser printer. While these cost more to purchase, they don't use ink, so won't dry out.

- If you're planning to print photos, consider getting an inkjet printer. They will produce more vibrant images, they're more affordable, and they're smaller too.

A typical laser printer

A typical inkjet printer

Add a USB printer

1 Use the instructions that came with your printer to unpack it, install ink or toner, and add paper. Next, turn on the printer and make sure there are no errors on its display.

2 Connect one end of the USB cable into the printer, then the other end into your Mac. If you see a message prompting you to download new software, make sure to download and install it.

Important: If the USB cable doesn't fit into your Mac, use a multiport adapter. You can purchase these in most electrical stores for around 20 dollars or pounds.

Add a Wi-Fi or network printer

If your Mac and printer are connected to the same Wi-Fi network, the printer might be available to use without any setup. To check, choose **File** > **Print**, click the **Printer** pop-up menu, choose **Nearby Printers**, then choose your printer. If your printer isn't available, then here's how to add it:

1. Use the instructions that came with your printer to unpack it, install ink or toner, and add paper. Next, turn on the printer and make sure there are no errors on its display.

2. Follow the instructions that came with the printer to connect it to your Wi-Fi network.

3. Open the **System Preferences** app, then click **Printers & Scanners**.

4. Click the **plus (+)** button at the bottom of the window. A dialogue will appear listing all the printers on your local network. It may take a moment for yours to appear. Select your printer when it appears, then click **Add**. If you see a message prompting you to download new software, make sure to download and install it.

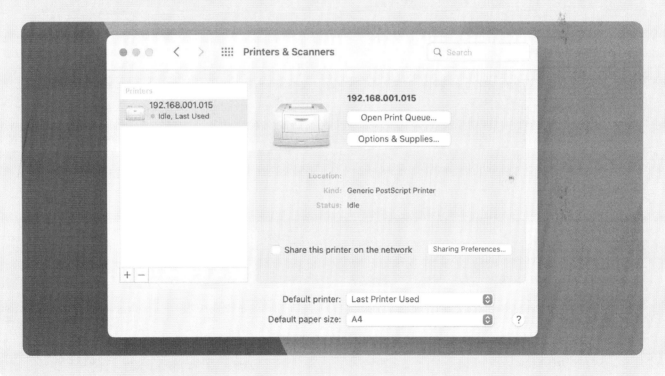

When you're ready to print

Click **File** in the menu at the top of the screen, then choose **Print**. You can also press **Command** > **P** on the keyboard. Next, use the print command window to select your printer, configure its output, then print.

Learn about Menus

Discover the basics of using menus on your Mac...

Unlike mobile operating systems such as iOS and Android, where icons and buttons are the primary methods of interacting with things, menus are an essential part of using your Mac. You'll need to use menus whenever you open or edit a file, interact with an app, or perform a task.

Apple menu bar icons explained

Take a look in the top-right corner of the screen and you'll see a number of icons. These all act as shortcuts to a number of services, such as Wi-Fi settings, the ability to search your Mac, or talk to Siri.

1 Get a detailed overview on your MacBook's current battery state. You can also get an idea of which apps are using significant battery charge.

2 Connect to Wi-Fi hotspots from this menu. You can also share your connection with other devices from this menu, or quickly jump to the Wi-Fi System Preferences panel.

3 If you have multiple user accounts set up on your Mac, then you can jump between them from this menu.

4 To search for anything on your Mac, such as files, folders, apps or settings, click the **search** icon in the menu.

5 Click this icon to open Control Centre, where you can manage basic settings with a single click.

6 Click the **Siri** icon in the top-right corner to ask your Mac to perform a task. You can find out more about Siri later in this chapter.

7 See the date and time from this menu option. If you click on these numbers, then you'll be able to see what notifications are awaiting you.

The Apple Menu

Turn on your Mac, look in the top-left corner and you'll see the Apple Menu. The Apple logo gives it away.

To use the Apple Menu, click on the **Apple** logo then choose an option. To close the menu, click anywhere outside the menu, or click on the Apple logo again.

Let's explore some of the shortcuts found in the Apple Menu:

About This Mac

Click on this option and you'll see a pop-up window displaying information about your Mac, including its software version, and hardware configuration.

System Preferences & App Store

Quickly access the preferences app for your Mac, or visit the App Store where you can discover millions of apps.

Recent Items

This menu option displays all of your recently opened apps, files, and folders.

Force Quit

If an app has crashed, click this shortcut in the Apple Menu to force-quit it.

Sleep, Restart and Shut Down

You can put your MacBook to sleep by closing its lid, but you can also use this menu option in the Apple Menu. Notice the other two shortcuts for restarting your Mac or shutting it down fully.

Lock Screen

If you're stepping away from your Mac and want to quickly lock it -- without putting it to sleep -- click this option. When you return to the Mac you will be asked to re-enter your password.

Control Centre

Adjust basic settings with just a single click...

Tucked away in the menu bar are a helpful set of buttons for toggling settings and activating features. They include a slider for controlling the screen brightness, a button for enabling Wi-Fi, toggle Do Not Disturb, and more. To access these buttons at any time, click on the **Control Centre** button (⬒) in the top-right corner of the menu.

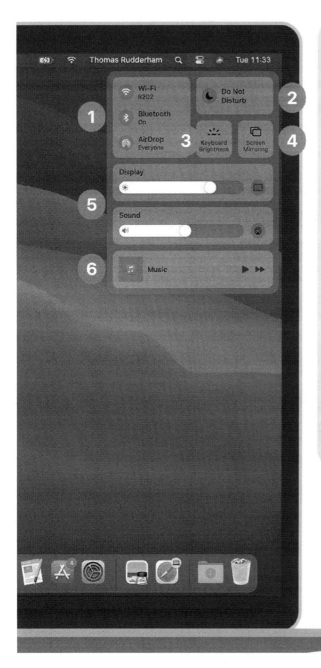

1 Toggle Wi-Fi, Bluetooth, or AirDrop on or off by clicking on their respective icons.

2 Click the **moon** icon to instantly toggle Do Not Disturb on or off. When enabled, you won't be interrupted by FaceTime calls, messages, or notifications.

3 You can adjust the keyboard backlight brightness by clicking this button.

4 Click on the **Screen Mirroring** button to share your Mac's display with an Apple TV connected to the same Wi-Fi network.

5 Use these two sliders to adjust the display brightness or audio volume level. You can also click on the small buttons to the right of each to access additional settings.

6 Control music playback using this panel at the bottom of Control Centre.

Additional controls

When you move the mouse cursor over a control, a small arrow appears on the right. Click this arrow, and you can access additional controls. Here are a couple of examples...

Wi-Fi settings

Click on the arrow to the right of the **Wi-Fi** button, and you'll see a toggle switch for disabling Wi-Fi, any additional Wi-Fi networks in the area, and a shortcut to Network Preferences.

Display settings

Similarly, if you click on the **Display** arrow, you'll see toggle switches for Dark Mode, Night Shift, True Tone, plus shortcut links to Display and Sidecar Preferences.

Add additional modules to Control Centre

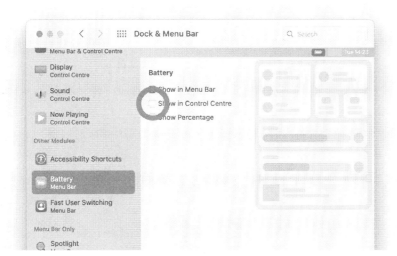

There are three additional modules that you can add to Control Centre:

- Accessibility Shortcuts
- Battery
- Fast User Switching

To add these modules, open **System Preferences**, then click **Dock & Menu Bar**. Scroll down the sidebar on the left, and you'll see shortcuts for each of these. To add them to Control Centre, simply click **Show in Control Centre**.

The Desktop

Learn how to use folders and organise your files...

Log into your Mac and the first place you visit is the Desktop. At the top of the Desktop is the Apple Menu, and at the bottom is the Dock, where all your favorite apps are located. Think of the Desktop as the home screen on your Mac. It's a place where you can leave folders, recent files and shortcuts to external drives. Or if you like to keep things tidy, nothing at all except a beautiful wallpaper.

An overview of a folder:

1 **Window controls.** See these small coloured gumdrops? You can use these to close, minimise/expand folders, apps, and windows.

2 **Navigation controls.** Go back or forward through your folders using these small arrows.

3 **View options.** These buttons change the look of your folders. On the left is the grid view, followed by list, columns, and Gallery.

4 **Options.** Click the options button to sort a folder's contents by kind, date, size, and tag.

5 **Share.** The Share button lets you send a folder to others via Mail, Messages, AirDrop, and more.

6 **Tags.** Add a tag colour to a file or folder using this button.

7 **Search.** If you need to find a specific file or document, click this bar then type your query.

8 **Sidebar.** The left-hand sidebar acts a shortcut to various folders and devices.

9 **Information.** This panel on the right provides information about files, such as their size, date, and tags. When you select the Gallery view (as seen here), then you can also access shortcuts to common tasks such as sharing files.

Resize a folder or window

To make a folder bigger or smaller, hover the cursor over any corner of the folder, then click and drag it. You'll see the folder resize as you move the cursor around the screen. This also applies to app windows such as Safari or Mail.

Files

Whenever you work with an app or save something from the web, the data you have interacted with is saved as a file on your Mac. Files are basically pieces of data that are saved together in a single collection, and they come in a mindbogglingly vast number of formats, such as:

.jpg - an image
.png - another type of image
.mov - a video file
.mp4 - another video file
.zip - a compressed file
.pages - a Pages file

Before applying Stack view

After applying Stack view

Use Stacks to organise your desktop files

By using the Stacks view you can automatically group all of the files on your desktop into sets. Let's say you have 10 jpg images, and 4 PDFs on your Desktop. When you use Stacks, those 10 images will be organised into a single stack, and there will be another stack containing the 4 PDFs. Here's how it works:

1. Click on **View** in the Finder menu, then choose **Use Stacks**.

2. You'll see all of your desktop files organise themselves into stacks.

3. To preview a stack of files, just hover the cursor over it, then perform the scroll gesture.

4. To open a stack, click on it. To close a stack, click away from it.

Discover apps

There's a whole world of apps available for your Mac...

Without any third-party apps, your Mac would basically be a glorified web browser. Thankfully, there are literally millions of apps available for you to install and enjoy, including photo editors, games, music production tools and more.

Before we get to third-party apps, let's explore the ones which are already installed on your Mac...

Launchpad

Every application and utility is stored in an area of the Desktop called Launchpad. It's a bit like the Home screen on an iPhone or iPad, enabling you to browse your apps, arrange them into folders and (if installed from the App Store), and even delete them.

The easiest way to access Launchpad at any time is to click the **Launchpad** icon in the Dock. It looks like a small collection of coloured cubes; and by default, it's located on the left-side of the Dock.

If you've removed Launchpad from the Dock then you can also access it by pinching closed your thumb and three fingers on the trackpad.

Add to Launchpad

Any app you download from the App Store is automatically added to Launchpad, as are any apps added to the Applications folder on your Mac. You can find a shortcut to the Applications folder in the sidebar of a folder.

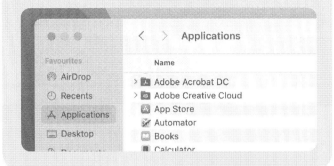

Search for an app

If you have a wealth of apps installed on your Mac and want to quickly find the right one, just start typing its name when you're viewing Launchpad and you'll automatically see it appear.

Organise your apps

Moving apps around Launchpad or re-organising them into folders is easy:

Re-arrange apps: Drag an app to a new location using the trackpad or mouse.

Create a folder: Simply drag an app on top of another.

Rename a folder: When viewing a folder click its name then enter a new one.

Delete an app from Launchpad

To delete an app, simply **click and hold** on the app icon, then when it starts to jiggle click the **X** icon. If you don't see the X icon appear, then the app was likely installed outside of the App Store. If it's the latter and you still want to delete the app:

1. Go to the Finder, click **Go** in the menu bar then choose **Applications**.

2. Drag the app icon or its folder to the **Trash** icon in the Dock.

3. Alternatively, right-click on the app or app folder then choose **Move to Trash**.

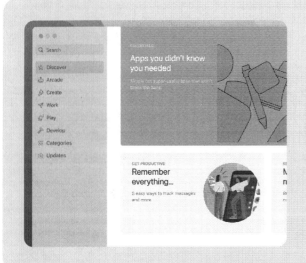

Check out the App Store

As you might have guessed, the App Store is the best place to find new and exciting apps for your Mac. It's updated constantly with the latest apps, updates and games; and because every app is approved by Apple, you don't have to worry about spam or hidden viruses.

To open the App Store on your Mac, just click on **Launchpad**, then click the **App Store** icon. You can also click on the **Apple** logo in the menu at the top of the screen, then choose **App Store**.

Install an app

When you're ready to install an app, click on its **price**, then the blue **Buy App** button. If the app is free, it works in the same way: just click **Get**, then the blue **Install App** button.

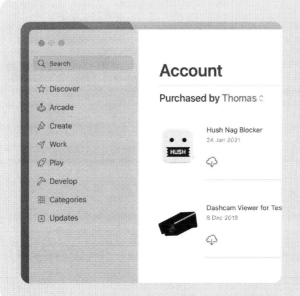

View your app purchases or redeem a promo code

When viewing the App Store on your Mac, click on your **profile** photo in the bottom-left corner. On the following screen you'll see every app purchase you've ever made, alongside free apps you've downloaded. To re-download an app click on the **cloud** icon.

From this screen you can also redeem a promo code. Just click the **Redeem Gift Card** button in the top-right corner then follow the on-screen prompts to enter the gift card's code.

Install apps from the web

So you've downloaded an app from the web. What next? The process of unpacking and installing a third-party application from the internet is slightly more complicated than using the App Store. Here's how it works:

1 Everything you download is saved to the Downloads folder. You can find this towards the right-side of the Dock. Alternatively, if you're on the Desktop click **Go** in the Finder menu, then choose **Downloads**.

2 Look for the application you've downloaded. If it's a zip file just double-click to unzip it.

3 Double-click on the unzipped file. If you get an error message that says "*This program can't be opened because it wasn't downloaded from the Mac App Store,*" don't worry, all you need to do is right-click on the file and select **Open**.

4 A folder will be mounted on the Desktop which contains an installation file. Double-click this file then follow the on-screen instructions to install the app.

5 Once the installation process has completed, close it then eject the mounted folder by either dragging it to the **Trash** or by clicking the **eject** button in the Finder window sidebar.

AxureRP-
Setup.dmg

Talk to Siri

Take command of your very own assistant...

Imagine Siri as your very own personal assistant. He (or she depending on your country of origin), can make FaceTime calls for you, dictate emails and messages, make a restaurant reservation, remind you to do things, tell you about movies, make jokes, and much more.

Siri isn't perfect, however. It can't remember interactions from the past, it relies on hearing your voice in a clear manner, and it needs a connection to the internet to work. If you're aware of these limitations and don't mind the odd false request, then Siri can save time and even be a little fun to use.

There are three ways to enable Siri:

1 Click the **Siri** icon in the Dock.

2 Press the **Siri** button in the top-right corner of the Touch bar.

3 Click the **Siri** icon in the top-right corner of the Apple Menu ( ).

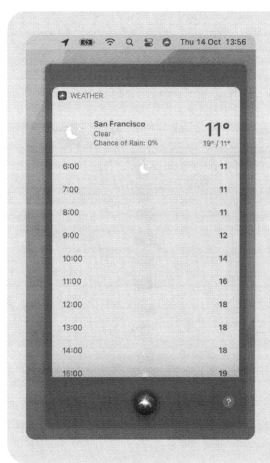

Speak to Siri

Next, say out loud, *"What's the weather like today?"* Siri will automatically look for a weather report then tell you what it's going to be like. It's that simple to use Siri.

Enable 'Type to Siri'

Sometimes it's not appropriate, or possible, to talk to Siri, so your Mac offers the option to type to Siri instead. To enable Type to Siri:

1 Click on the **Apple** menu, then **System Preferences.**

2 Click on the **Accessibility** option, then scroll down the sidebar and choose **Siri.**

3 Click the **Enable Type to Siri** checkbox. Now, when you activate Siri, you'll see a text box. Type a query and press Enter on your keyboard to use it.

Activate Siri with a shortcut

To activate Siri using the keyboard, press **Command-Space**. To use a different keyboard shortcut:

1 Click on the **Apple** menu then **System Preferences**.

2 Click on the **Siri** option.

3 Under **Keyboard Shortcut**, use the drop-down menu to select another option. You can choose from Command-Space (default), Option-Space, Function-Space, or you can create your own keyboard shortcut.

Things you can ask Siri...

"Play something by Monsters and Men."

"Remind me to call Michael at 7."

"Send a message to Dave."

"Set up a meeting with Sarah at 9."

"Email Chris to say I'm running late."

"Show me movies directed by Steven Spielberg."

"Find the files I worked on yesterday."

"Put the Mac to sleep."

Use AirDrop to share files

Send photos or files to friends nearby...

Whenever you need to share a file with another Mac, iPhone, or iPad, AirDrop is the answer. It works by sending files to other Apple devices within a 30 feet radius. You can send anything you like, from photos, videos, or files; and the devices don't need to share the same Apple ID, so you can share files with nearly anyone, so long as they have an Apple device.

Send a file

To share a file from the Finder, click on **Go** in the menu at the top of the screen, then choose **AirDrop**. You can also use the keyboard shortcut **Shift-Command-R**.

You'll see the AirDrop Finder window open and display any devices that are within reach. To send a file, simply drag and drop it onto the device. If the device has a different Apple ID, then the owner will need to approve the transfer; otherwise the file will automatically be transferred and opened.

Share a file using an app

If you want to share something in an app, like a webpage in Safari, or a document in Pages, click the **Share** icon (it looks like a square with an arrow pointing up), then choose **AirDrop** from the menu. You can then use the AirDrop window to share the file.

Control who can see your Mac

If you're in a public space and don't want others to see your Mac in AirDrop, open the AirDrop panel via the Finder, click on the blue piece of text that says "*Allow me to be discovered by: Everyone*", and choose from either people in your contacts list, or no-one.

If you can't see someone...

If they are using an iPad or iPhone, ask them to open the AirDrop panel in Control Centre, then enable AirDrop.

If they are using a Mac, ask them to open the AirDrop window via the Finder and they should appear.

44

Use AirPlay to stream content

Send video and music to your TV, or even your Mac's entire screen...

With AirPlay you can wirelessly stream content to an Apple TV, or play music over AirPlay speakers such as HomePod. All you need to do is connect your Mac to the same Wi-Fi connection shared with your AirPlay devices; there are no complicated configurations to set up, all the hard work is done for you.

What you can stream over AirPlay:
- Music and Beats 1 Radio

What you can stream to an Apple TV:
- Movies and videos
- Music and Beats 1 Radio
- Photos and slideshows
- Your entire Mac display

Stream content to your Apple TV

Whenever you're listening to music or watching a video and want to stream it to an Apple TV, click the **AirPlay** button, then select your Apple TV. It looks like a square with an up arrow in the lower-middle.

If you don't see the AirPlay button, chances are the app or website doesn't support AirPlay streaming.

Mirror your Mac on an Apple TV

If you want to show your Mac's display on an Apple TV, click the **Control Panel** button in the top-right corner of the menu menu, choose **Screen Mirroring**, then select the Apple TV.

When AirPlay is active, the menu bar will turn blue to let you know.

How to use Spotlight

Learn how to find files, hide folders and more...

Think of Spotlight as Google, but instead of searching the web you're searching your Mac. Using Spotlight you can pretty much search for anything you can think of. Files, emails, apps, music tracks, contacts, and even information within documents.

That's not all, because Spotlight does a pretty good job of replacing Google too, so you can use it to search for Wikipedia information, flight times, sports results, and more.

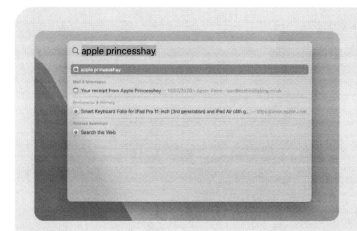

Access Spotlight

It's easy, just click on the **magnifying glass** icon in the menu bar at the top of the screen, then start typing a search query.

You can search for things like "apple store" or "emails from Sam". You can also open Spotlight using the keyboard shortcut: command-space.

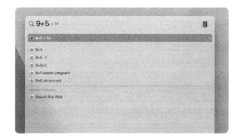

Calculations and conversions

To calculate something, type "5+5" into Spotlight.

To convert something, type "20 feet to metres".

To see the definition of a word, type it then click the result in the Definition section.

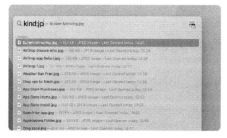

Search for a specific type of file

To search for a specific type of file, type "kind:" then the type of file. For example, you can search for "kind:jpg", "kind:folder", or "kind:video".

See a file's location on your Mac

To see the location of a file on your Mac, click on the search result, then press and hold the **Command** key. The file's location will then appear in the bottom of the Spotlight window. To open the location, press **Command-R**.

Customise search results

If Spotlight doesn't find what you're looking for, or if you want to limit where it should and shouldn't be searching, then here's how you can customise search results:

1 Click on the **Apple** menu button on the top-left of your screen.

2 Click **System Preferences**.

3 Click on **Spotlight**.

4 Un-tick items to hide them from Spotlight results, or tick them to show them.

Hide a folder from Spotlight

If you want to hide a folder from Spotlight results:

1 Open **System Preferences** and click on **Spotlight**.

2 Click the **Privacy** tab.

3 Click the **plus** icon in the lower-left corner, then select a folder. It will now be hidden from Spotlight results.

4 You can also drag a folder to this panel.

Notifications and Widgets

Discover how to manage notifications and widgets...

Notifications on your Mac let you know about updates, new messages, and other activities going within apps and the operating system. There are typically two ways a notification might appear on your Mac:

● **Notification alerts**
Whenever your Mac or an app wants to let you know about something, a small notification window will appear in the top-right corner of the screen. You might see that an update is available, or it could be a new message from a friend.

● **App badges**
If you see a small red dot above the app icon in your Dock, then the app is letting you know that a new message or update is awaiting.

You can also see all of your notifications in one place: Notification Centre. From here you can see all your app notifications, missed calls, calendar events, and messages. You can also access widgets from here. These are small panels of information, such as the latest stocks or weather.

Access Notification Centre

To open Notification Centre, click the **date and time** in the very top-right corner of your screen. You can also use a two-finger swipe from right to left, starting at the right edge of your Mac's trackpad.

When you open Notification Centre, you'll see a number of widgets running down the side of the screen. These are designed to quickly provide information at a glance, but you can click on each of them to open the corresponding app. For example, if you click on a Message notification, then the Messages app will open.

Add or remove widgets

When you open Notification Centre you'll see a small number of widgets, including the weather and stocks. To add more widgets, remove widgets or rearrange them:

- **To remove widgets:** Click **Edit Widgets** at the bottom of the screen, then click on the **minus** button which appears over the widget.

- **To add widgets:** Move the cursor over the widget you'd like to add, then click the **green plus** button which appears

- **To rearrange widgets:** Click and hold on a widget, then drag it to its new location.

Customise notification alerts

If an app is constantly sending your alerts, or you want to customise how alerts appear on your Mac, then here's how you can disable or edit them:

1. Open **System Preferences,** then choose **Notifications**.

2. Select an app from the sidebar. You can then choose from banner alerts, small alerts or none.

3. You can also disable badge icons and sounds for each app.

Reply to a message from a notification

If a message notification appears while you're using your Mac, click the **Show More** button and you'll be able to send a reply without going into the Messages app.

How to cut, copy, and paste

Discover how to copy something then paste it somewhere else...

Copying and pasting is a great way to move text or content from one app to another. For example, you could copy your address from Contacts then paste it into Safari, or copy a photo from the internet and then paste it into an email. Here's how it works...

Copy text

Find a source of text on your Mac, perhaps your phone number in Contacts. **Right-click** on the number, then choose **Copy** from the pop-up menu. You can also press **Command-C** on the keyboard.

Paste text

Next, close Contacts and open the Notes app. Create a new note or select an existing one, **right-click** within the note and choose **Paste**. You can also press **Command-V** on the keyboard.

Copy images

To copy an image from the internet, open Safari, find an image on any website, **right-click** on it and choose **Copy Image**. You can now paste this image into a new email, message, note, or graphic-based app.

Copy and paste between Mac and iPhone or iPad

Copying and pasting is a great way to quickly move content from one app to another. With just a few clicks it's possible to copy text in Notes then paste it into Safari, or copy an image from the web and paste it into an email. However, it's also possible to copy content from one Apple device to another. For example, let's copy an website address from Safari on your Mac, then paste it into Safari on an iPhone.

1 Start by opening Safari on your Mac, then go to www.apple.com. Next, **right-click** on the website address bar at the top of the browser window and choose **Copy** in the pop-up window.

2 Next, using your iPhone, open the Safari app. Tap on the address field at the top of the screen, clear it by tapping the small **x** button, then **double-tap** on the address bar. In the small pop-up field, tap **Paste** and you'll see www.apple.com instantly appear in the address field.

This process of copying content from one device to another works seamlessly on iPhone, iPad and the Mac, but with one caveat: you need to be signed into the same Apple ID on every device.

Use Handoff to work between devices

Start something on your Mac, then continue it on your iPad or iPhone...

Most people won't have heard about Handoff. It's a rather clever feature which lets you start something on your Mac, then continue it on an iPad or iPhone. Take writing an email for example. You might begin to compose an email on your Mac, then later finish it on the go using your iPhone; or maybe you start reading a web page on your Mac, then continue it on an iPad. Here's how it works:

Turn Handoff on

To enable Handoff on your Mac, open **System Preferences**, click **General**, then ensure **Allow Handoff between this Mac and your iCloud devices** is ticked.

To enable Handoff on your iPhone and iPad, go to **Settings** > **General** > **Handoff & Suggested Apps**, then toggle the **Handoff** switch on.

Jump from iPhone to Mac

It's easy to swap tasks between an iPhone and Mac. Take reading a web page for example. When you open a web page on your iPhone, a Safari icon will appear on the left-side of the Dock on the Mac.

Just click on this icon to open the same webpage on your Mac. This same process goes for composing Notes, Emails and Messages, or adding Calendar and Contact entries.

Use Apple Pay to buy things

Leave your wallet in the drawer...

Apple Pay is pretty remarkable. You can use it to pay for apps and music with your Mac, or buy items online without entering your credit card details.

What is Apple Pay?

It's a way of paying for things by holding your iPhone or Apple Watch near a contactless payment terminal. On a Mac, you can use it online to pay for goods, or within apps when you see the Apple Pay logo, which looks like this:

Enable Apple Pay on your Mac

1. Open the **System Preferences** app, click on **Wallet & Apple Pay**, then follow the steps to add a card. If you're trying to add a card which already exists within your Apple ID account, then you'll only need to enter its security code.

2. Click **Next** and your bank will authorise and add your card. If your bank needs more details you can add these later via **System Preferences** > **Wallet & Apple Pay**.

Use Apple Pay online

If a website supports Apple Pay, you'll see a button at the checkout with the words "Check Out with Apple Pay". Click this button to make the purchase immediately using your Apple Pay account.

Use Apple Pay in an app

If you're using an app and see the Apple Pay logo, you might need to toggle a setting that enables Apple Pay first, the app will let you know. Once enabled, click the **Apple Pay** button, ensure all the details are correct, then use Touch ID to confirm your identity.

Add or remove credit cards

1. Open the **System Preferences** app, then select **Wallet & Apple Pay.**

2. To add a new credit card, click the **plus (+)** button below the sidebar.

3. To remove a card, select it using the sidebar then click the **minus (-)** button below the sidebar.

See your recent transactions

Every time you use Apple Pay the last few transactions will be stored as virtual receipts on your Mac. To see these:

1. Open the **System Preferences** app, then select **Wallet & Apple Pay.**

2. Click the **Transactions** tab at the top of the panel.

Magic Mouse gestures

There's more to the Magic Mouse than just clicking...

A Magic Mouse doesn't come included with the MacBook, but it's a worthwhile purchase for anyone who plans to use their Mac for productive purposes. That's because a mouse is far more accurate than a trackpad for manipulating small interface elements such as buttons and per-pixel-sized objects.

It's also packed with clever technologies, including a large touch-sensitive area on the top, which enables gestures to be used to scroll, zoom, and navigate through content:

Secondary Click

Press firmly on the right side of the Magic Mouse and you'll perform a secondary click, also known as a right-click. This action enables you to access shortcut menus or secondary features.

If the secondary click feature is disabled on your Mac, open the **System Preferences** app, select **Mouse**, then toggle **Secondary Click** on.

Scroll

To scroll through web pages or documents, slowly swipe your finger up and down the middle of the mouse. By flicking your finger you can scroll quicker.

If you don't like the direction in which scroll works, then you can flip it vertically. To do this open the **System Preferences** app, select **Mouse**, then toggle **Scroll Direction: Natural** off.

Swipe between pages

If you're using Safari and want to go back a page, just swipe your finger across the top of the mouse from left to right. You can also go forward by swiping right to left.

This isn't turned on by default, so to enable this feature open the **System Preferences** app, select **Mouse**, click the **More Gestures** tab, then enable **Swipe between pages**.

Swipe between full-screen apps

If you prefer to run your apps in full-screen mode, then you can quickly jump from one app to another by swiping left or right across the mouse with two fingers.

Quickly access Mission Control

Double-tap on the mouse with two fingers and you'll jump into Mission Control, which displays all your apps and windows on one screen.

Enable Smart Zoom

Smart Zoom lets you zoom into content by tapping twice on the top of the mouse. To enable this feature open the **System Preferences** app, select **Mouse**, then toggle **Smart Zoom** on.

Adjust the tracking speed

If you find that the mouse cursor moves too quickly or slowly, then it's possible to adjust the tracking speed to something more comfortable. To do this:

1 Open the **System Preferences** app, then select **Mouse.**

2 Look for the **Tracking Speed** slider, in the bottom half of the panel.

3 Drag the small slider button right to increase the tracking speed, or left to slow it down.

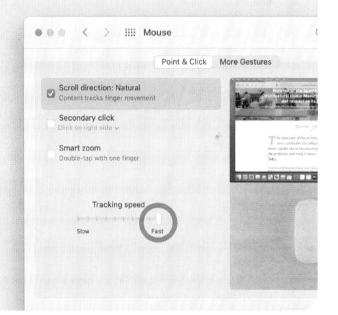

Mouse settings

Scroll and click how you like...

You might think of the mouse as something that's uncompromising; something that hasn't changed in decades, with no options for personalisation. As it turns out, the Magic Mouse is quite the opposite. It has a touch sensor on the top panel, enabling you to perform basic gestures, while its scrolling speed and direction can be tweaked to suit your preferences.

Make the mouse cursor bigger

If you often find yourself struggling to find the mouse cursor, then it's possible to make it larger using an accessibility setting. Here's how:

1. Open the **System Preferences** app, then select **Accessibility**.

2. Select **Display** in the sidebar, click the **Cursor** tab, then use the **Cursor size** slider to increase the size of the mouse cursor.

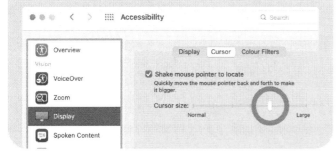

Change the scroll direction

By default, when you scroll a page using the mouse, it moves in the opposite direction, so to move the page down, you scroll up. If you find this confusing and would like to scroll the "natural" way, then:

1. Open the **System Preferences** app, then choose **Mouse**.

2. Tick the box for **Scrolling direction: Natural** to make the mouse scroll the same direction as your finger.

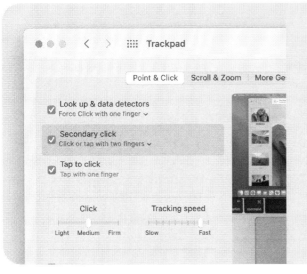

Enable secondary click

Secondary click works how you might imagine, assigning the right side of your mouse as a secondary (or right) click. Once activated, you can perform shortcuts and access secondary functions across the entirety of your Mac.

To enable right-click functionality, open the **System Preferences** app, choose **Mouse**, then enable the **Secondary click** option.

Adjust the double-click

To adjust how quickly your Mac recognises a double-click:

1 Open the **System Preferences** app, then select **Accessibility**.

2 Select **Pointer Control** in the sidebar.

3 Drag the **Double-click speed** slider to the right to increase how quickly you would like to double-click, or to the left to decrease it.

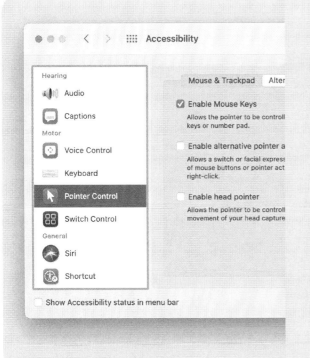

Use a keyboard to control the mouse cursor

If you have trouble controlling the mouse then it's possible to use the number keys on a keyboard to move the cursor and select things. To do this:

1 Open the **System Preferences** app, then select **Accessibility**.

2 Select **Pointer Control** in the sidebar, then click the **Alternative Control Methods** tab.

3 Click **Enable Mouse Keys**.

Now, when you press the number keys on your keyboard, the cursor will move. To click the mouse button, press **5**.

Trackpad gestures

Find out how to scroll, zoom and more...

It might not be obvious, but the large trackpad beneath the keyboard of your MacBook supports Multi-Touch gestures; just like the iPhone and iPad. Admittedly, it's not quite as intuitive as a touchscreen device, because there's no direct contact between your fingertip and the screen, but nevertheless, with a little practice, you'll soon be swiping between pages, zooming into photos, and scrolling through lists with ease.

The trick to using the trackpad is to practice with both fingers whenever you get the chance. You'll soon learn which gestures use one finger, which use two, and which even use three. You'll also learn how to move your fingers gently and smoothly across the trackpad.

Enable Multi-Touch gestures

Basic gestures are already enabled when you activate your Mac, but some of the advanced gestures, such as Look up data detectors, need to be manually activated. To do this, open the **System Preferences** app (or choose **Apple > System Preferences**) and then click **Trackpad**. On the following panel you can enable or disable specific gestures and watch instructional videos for each.

Single Click
The entire trackpad on your Mac acts as a button, so you can press down anywhere to "click", activate apps and select items.

Secondary Click
To enable right-click functionality, open the **System Preferences** app, choose **Trackpad**, then enable the **Secondary click** option. Now, whenever you tap on an item with two fingers, you'll activate secondary clicking.

Scroll through pages
If you want to scroll through a document or web page, place two fingers on the trackpad and move them up and down.

Zoom in and out

Place two fingers on the trackpad then pinch them apart to zoom in, or pinch them together to zoom out.

Rotate images

To rotate an image clockwise or anti-clockwise, place two fingers on the trackpad then twist them left or right. This is a tricky gesture so hard to perfect.

Force click

Your trackpad can tell when you tap lightly or tap firmly. That means if you press hard on a link in Safari you can preview the page, or if you press hard on a folder or file you can rename it.

Open Mission Control

To open the macOS Mission Control window place three fingers on the trackpad and move them quickly upwards. You'll then see all your windows slide into a tidy grid.

Go back a page in Safari

If you're browsing the web and want to go back a page, swipe from the left to the right with two fingers on the trackpad. Similarly, to go forward a page, swipe right to left.

Access App Expose

Swipe down the trackpad with three fingers and you'll see App Expose appear, letting you jump between windows with a tap.

Go to Launchpad

If you place your thumb and two fingers on the trackpad, then pinch them together, you'll instantly access Launchpad.

Swap between apps

Quickly jump between your open apps by placing three fingers on the trackpad then swiping left or right.

Access Notification Centre

To see your notifications at any time, swipe left from the right edge of the trackpad with two fingers.

Trackpad settings

Scroll, swipe, and click how you like...

The MacBook's trackpad is likely to be one of the best trackpads in the world. It's super sensitive, can support Multi-Touch gestures, and can simulate a "click" using haptic feedback. It's also easy to customise to suit your needs...

An overview of the Trackpad settings panel

To fully customise your Mac's trackpad, open the **System Preferences** app, then click on the **Trackpad** option.

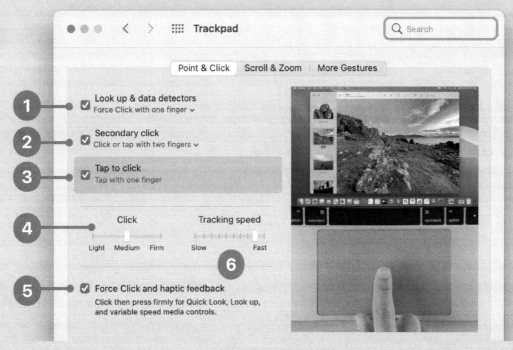

1 Look up & data detectors
With this enabled, you can select a word or a link, then tap on it with three fingers to show information about the word, or see a preview of the link.

2 Secondary link
Turn this on, and you can simulate a "right-click", by tapping on the trackpad with two fingers.

3 Tap to click
Turn this on, and you can click on things by lightly tapping on the trackpad.

4 Click strength
You can use this slider to adjust how hard you need to press on the trackpad to initiate a click.

5 Force Click and haptic feedback
Turn this on, and you can press and hold on something to see more information about it.

6 Tracking speed
This slider determines how quickly the pointer moves around the screen. You can make the trackpad more sensitive by moving the slider to the right, or less sensitive by moving it to the left.

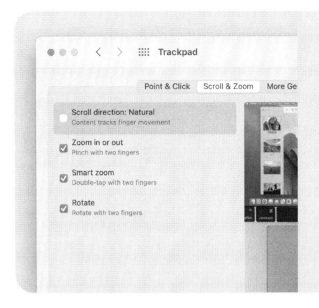

Invert the scroll direction

By default, when you scroll through content (such as a web page) using two fingers, the content will follow the direction of your fingers. This mimics the way touchscreens work, making it a natural way to navigate through content.

If you'd prefer to invert the scrolling direction, so pages scroll downwards when you swipe up, click on the **Scroll & Zoom** tab at the top of the Trackpad settings panel, then untick **Scroll direction: Natural**.

Customise trackpad gestures

While exploring the Trackpad settings panel, click the **More Gestures** tab to discover a number of trackpad gestures (see the previous two pages for an overview of each gesture).

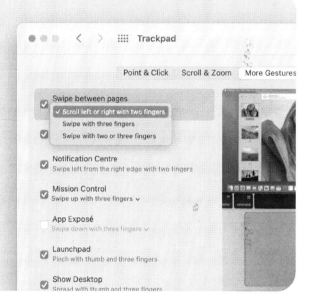

On this panel, you can customise how gestures are initiated. To do this, click the small dropdown arrow to the right of the gesture. You'll then see a handful of options.

Keyboard shortcuts

Discover how to quickly perform actions using the keyboard...

Long before touch screen technology or the mouse came along, the keyboard was king. It was the primary way to interact with any type of computer, whether it was a Mac, a Windows PC, or an IBM machine; so inevitably, a huge number of keyboard shortcuts were devised to save precious time.

Using keyboard shortcuts it's possible to copy and paste, take a screenshot, swap between apps, hide a window and much more. The following two pages will reveal all of these essential shortcuts, plus a few more that will save time and make your Mac even more productive.

The basics

See the button next to the spacebar on your Mac? It should have a looped square symbol in the top corner, then the word *Command* underneath. This is the Command key and it acts as a shortcut for a number of tasks. Take quitting an app for example. If, at any time, you want to quickly quit the current app, press the **Command** key, keep holding it down, then press **Q**. You'll then see the app instantly quit. This method of holding the Command key, then pressing another key, is used for a wide range of tasks.

Common commands

Command-Q: Quit the current app.

Command-A: Select everything on the screen or within a window.

Command-F: Find items within a document. If you're in the Finder you can search your Mac.

Command-O: Open a new file, or a selected file.

Command-S: Save your work or file.

Command-W: Close the current window.

Command-H: Hide the current app or window.

Command-P: Print the current window or page.

Command-Z: Undo whatever action you've just done.

Command-Shift-Z: Redo the Undo action.

Command-Spacebar: Opens Spotlight.

Command-Tab: Switch between open apps.

Option-Command-Esc: Force quit an app.

Command-Shift-3: Take a screenshot.

Command-Shift-4: Capture a specific part of the screen.

Command-Shift-4-Space: Capture the current window or view.

Spacebar: Select a file then press Spacebar to preview it. This includes PDFs, videos, images and more.

Sleep, power and log out

Power button: Press to put your Mac to sleep. Hold down for 1.5 seconds to display a dialog asking if you would like to sleep, restart or shut down. Hold for 5 seconds to force your Mac to shutdown.

Shift-Command-Q: Log out of your user account.

Option-Shift-Command-Q: Log out of your account.

Copy and paste

Copying and pasting is a great way to copy text and content from one app to another. You're basically making a duplicate of the original thing. For example, you could copy your address from the Contacts app, then paste it into Safari; or you could copy a photo from the web and then paste it into an email. The options are endless.

Copy something: Select a file then press **Command-C** to copy it. Alternatively, right-click on it and choose **Copy** in the pop-up window.

Paste something: Next, go to where you want to copy whatever you've selected, then press **Command-V** to paste it. Alternatively, you can right-click and choose **Paste** from the pop-up window. You'll see the text, photo, file or folder appear.

Finder commands

Command-D: Duplicate selected file/s.

Command-E: Eject the selected disk or volume.

Command-I: Show the Get Info window for a selected file.

Shift-Command-C: Open the Computer window.

Shift-Command-D: Open the Desktop folder.

Shift-Command-F: Open the All My Files.

Shift-Command-G: Open a Go to Folder window.

Shift-Command-H: Go to the Home folder.

Shift-Command-I: Open your iCloud Drive.

Shift-Command-K: Open the Network window.

Option-Command-L: Open your Downloads folder.

Shift-Command-O: Open the Documents folder.

Shift-Command-R: Open the AirDrop window.

Control-Shift-Command-T: Add a selected Finder item to the Dock.

Shift-Command-U: Open the Utilities folder.

Control-Command-T: Add the selected item to the sidebar.

Command-J: Show View Options.

Command-K: Open the Connect to Server window.

Command-L: Make an alias of a selected item.

Command-N: Open a new Finder window.

Shift-Command-N: Create a new folder.

Option-Command-N: Create a new Smart Folder.

Command-R: Show the original file for an alias.

Command-Y: Use Quick Look to preview a file.

Command-1: View items in the Finder as icons.

Command-2: View items in the Finder as a list.

Command-3: View items in the Finder as columns.

Command-4: View items in the Finder with Cover Flow.

Command–Mission Control: Show the desktop.

Option–double-click: Open a folder in a separate window.

Command–double-click: Open a folder in a separate tab or window.

Command-Delete: Move item to the Trash.

Shift-Command-Delete: Empty the Trash.

Special characters, accents and symbols

Learn how to find emojis, symbols, and more...

Every now and then you might need to enter a special character in a document, or within an app. It might be an accent used by a foreign language, such as an acute symbol, a diaeresis, or an underbar.

Finding these characters on your keyboard can be tricky, because they're not always labeled, but thankfully, it's really easy to explore and apply these accents: just hold down the corresponding letter, then choose the correct accent via the pop-up field. Here's what it looks like when you hold down the e character when typing an email:

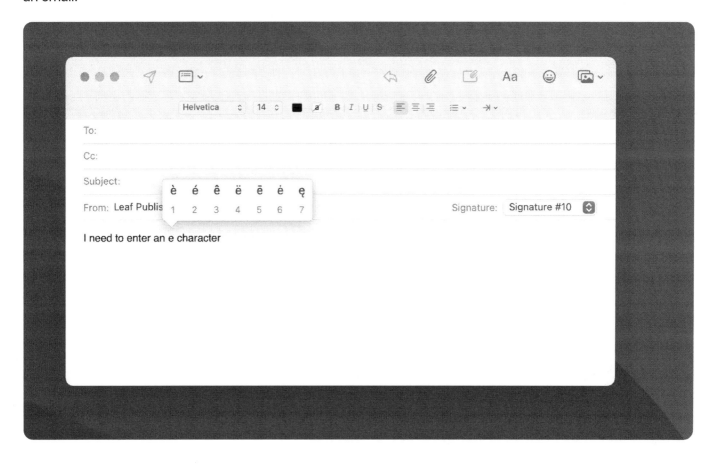

Shortcuts

If you would like to enter special characters and symbols, here are the shortcuts you need to type:

?: Shift-/

!: Shift-1

@: Shift-2

£: Shift-3

$: Shift-4

€: Option-3

%: Shift-5

&: Shift-7

*: Shift-8

#: Option-3

∞: Option-5

•: Option-8

©: Option-G

®: Option-R

™: Shift-Option-2

** **: Shift-Option-K

π: Option-P

ø: Option-O

Use the Character Viewer to insert symbols, emoji, and punctuation

If you'd like to explore all the characters, accents, symbols and pictographs available on your Mac, or if you're looking for something very specific, then the Character Viewer is a great tool for searching and inserting characters.

To display the Character Viewer, click the place within a document or message where you want the character to appear, then press **Control–Command–Spacebar**. The Character Viewer will then appear. Click the icon in the top-right corner to expand it like this:

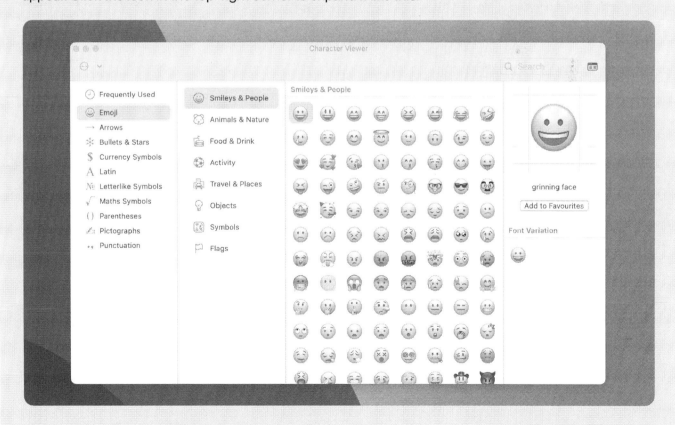

When you find the character you need, just click on it to insert it into your document or message.

Touch Bar basics

Discover how to use the touchscreen above the keyboard...

Introduced alongside the 2016 MacBook Pro, but later dropped in 2021, the Touch Bar is a thin touchscreen that runs along the top of the MacBook Pro keyboard. Given its five year run, there are a lot of MacBook's out there with a Touch Bar, so the next few pages will explain the basics behind it, how to use it, and how to customise its layout.

The Touch Bar is context-sensitive, which means it will change in realtime depending on what you're doing at any given moment. So when navigating the Desktop, the Touch Bar will show shortcuts for sharing and tagging files. Open multiple tabs in Safari, and you'll see thumbnails for each across the Touch Bar. It's also fully customisable, so you can rearrange buttons and even add your own shortcuts, as we'll discover over the next few pages.

The basics

When you first turn on your MacBook Pro, the Touch Bar displays familiar buttons like the Escape key, brightness and volume controls and Siri:

See the small white arrow to the left of the brightness control? By tapping this an additional row of shortcuts will expand into view, like this:

You can tap any of these shortcut to perform an action.

Function Keys

To use the F1–F12 function buttons in the Touch Bar, hold the **Function** (fn) key in the bottom-left corner of your keyboard. The function keys then appear:

Adjust the volume or brightness

When you want to quickly adjust the brightness or volume levels, place your finger on one of the buttons then immediately slide it left or right:

Turn the Touch Bar back on

After a period of inactivity your Touch Bar will turn off or dim the backlight. To turn it back on, just tap it with your finger.

Use the Touch Bar in apps

The Touch Bar is constantly adapting to your actions and the apps running on your screen. Here are a few examples of how it can be used in a variety of apps:

Finder:

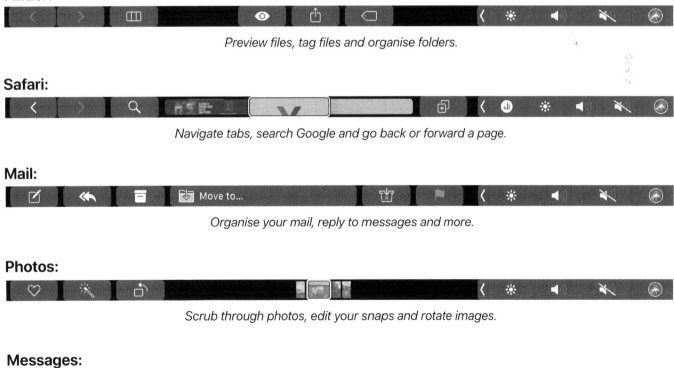

Preview files, tag files and organise folders.

Safari:

Navigate tabs, search Google and go back or forward a page.

Mail:

Organise your mail, reply to messages and more.

Photos:

Scrub through photos, edit your snaps and rotate images.

Messages:

Insert emojis or predictive text using the Touch Bar.

Customise the Touch Bar

Rearrange keys to suit your needs and workflow...

Because the Touch Bar isn't a fixed set of hardware keys, you can configure it to work in a number of ways. For example, you can rearrange the layout of buttons, show expanded controls, or toggle the traditional Function Keys.

Customise the Touch Bar view

Many apps such as Finder, Safari and Messages allow you to edit the Touch Bar shortcuts and actions. Here's how it works:

1. When using an app, go to **View > Customise Touch Bar**.

2. The Touch Bar Customise view will take over the screen, while below on the Touch Bar, all the buttons will start to wiggle.

3. Use your cursor to drag items from the display down onto the Touch Bar.

4. You can rearrange items within the Touch Bar by dragging them around.

5. You can also remove items from the Touch Bar by dragging them up and off the Touch Bar.

6. Tap the **Done** button on the Touch Bar to confirm your changes, or click **Done** on the screen.

Show expanded control shortcuts all the time

Look at the Touch Bar and you'll see a small white arrow pointing left. By tapping this you can access a number of controls and shortcuts for brightness and volume, media playback, and Launchpad. This panel of shortcuts is called the Control Strip. If you would like to always display the Control Strip on the Touch Bar:

1 Open the **System Preferences** app, then select **Keyboard**.

2 Click on the **Touch Bar shows** drop-down and select **Expanded Control Strip**.

Show the Function Keys all the time

If you're used to seeing F1, F2, etc on your keyboard, then it's possible to disable the adaptable Touch Bar view and use the function keys instead. To do this open the **System Preferences** app, select **Keyboard**, then click on the **Touch Bar shows** drop-down and select **F1, F2, etc. Keys**.

Customise the Control Strip

To rearrange the Control Strip shortcuts, remove shortcuts or add even more:

1 Open the **System Preferences** app, select **Keyboard**, then click **Customise Control Strip...**

2 The screen will blur and the buttons on the Touch Bar will start to wiggle. Notice that the Control Strip is set to minimise view, with the (<) button showing.

3 You can rearrange items within the Control Strip by dragging them around with the cursor.

4 You can remove items by dragging them up and off the bar. To add items, drag them down from the screen above.

5 Click **Done** when you're finished.

Change the desktop wallpaper

Give the Desktop background a fresh coat of paint...

One of the easiest ways to customise your Mac is to change the desktop wallpaper image. There are dozens to choose from, and you can even use a photo of your own. To get started:

Change the wallpaper:

1 Right-click on the current desktop wallpaper, then choose **Change Desktop Background**.

2 Alternatively, open the **System Preferences** app, then click on **Desktop & Screen Saver**.

3 Click on **Desktop Pictures** to choose an image supplied by Apple.

4 Choose **Colours** if you'd like to apply a sold colour background to your desktop.

5 Alternatively, click on any of the options under **Photos** or **Folders** to choose a personal image saved on your Mac.

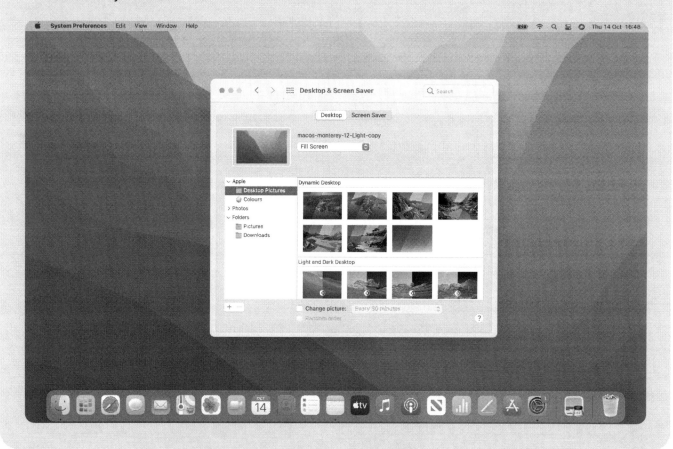

Use a dynamic wallpaper

A dynamic wallpaper will change its appearance to suit the time of day. So when you turn on your Mac in the morning you'll see sunlit dunes, while at night you'll see them lit by the stars. To enable this subtle but evocative wallpaper:

1 Open the **System Preferences** app, then click on **Desktop & Screen Saver**.

2 Click on **Desktop Pictures**, then look for the images labelled as **Dynamic Desktop**.

Automatically change wallpapers

You can ask your Mac to automatically change the wallpaper on a regular basis. To do this go to the **Desktop & Screen Saver** panel, select a photo-based image from the **Desktop Pictures** area, then tick **Change picture**. You can then use the drop-down to select a time duration, anywhere from every 5 seconds, to once a day.

Use a screen saver

Lock and hide the desktop, but leave the screen on while you're away...

A screen saver is an animated sequence that plays out across the display whenever you're not using it. There are a few advantages to running a screensaver while you're not using the Mac:

- It's a helpful way to remind yourself that the Mac is still running.
- It prevents anyone else from seeing what's on the screen when you're not there.
- It can prevent "burn-in" from happening. This is where a stationery item (such as the dock or menu), becomes burned into the screen when it has been displayed for a long period of time. Don't worry however, as this only happens on older external displays.

Set up a screen saver:

1 Right-click on the current desktop wallpaper, choose **Change Desktop Background**, then when the **Desktop & Screen Saver** panel appears, click the **Screen Saver** tab.

2 Alternatively, open the **System Preferences** app, click on **Desktop & Screen Saver,** then click **Screen Saver**.

Select a screen saver

From the **Desktop & Screen Saver** panel, look in the left-hand side of it and you'll see several screen savers to choose from.

Click on a screen saver to select it, and see an animated preview on the right.

Customise a screen saver

From the **Desktop & Screen Saver** panel, select a screen saver from the left-hand side. You can use the drop-down menu below the preview to select a source of images, or to customise the screen saver.

Activate by using the "Hot Corner"

By assigning a corner of the screen as a "Hot Corner", you can activate the screen saver at any time by moving the cursor into that corner. Here's how it works:

1. Select a screen saver, then click the **Hot Corner...** button in the bottom-right corner.

2. In the pop-up window, select a corner of the screen, then use the drop-down menu to select **Start Screen Saver**. Click **OK** to save your preference.

3. To activate the screen saver, move the cursor into the corner you've chosen, and it will begin.

Use Mission Control

Arrange your working space across multiple desktops...

If you use your Mac for multiple distinct purposes (such as work and home), then it's a good idea to start using Mission Control. It works by enabling you to create multiple desktops, called *spaces*, to organise your apps and windows. By doing this, you can create a space for work apps and folders, and a space for your personal life.

How to activate Mission Control

There are many ways you can activate Mission Control:

- Press the **F3** button on the MacBook Air keyboard.
- Press the **function** key, then **F3** on the MacBook Pro Touch Bar.
- Swipe up with three fingers across the trackpad.
- Click on the **Launchpad** icon in the Dock, then open **Mission Control**.

After activating Mission Control, you'll see all the apps and windows open on your Mac:

Jump between spaces

To jump from one desktop space to another, open **Mission Control** then click on the space at the top of the screen:

Add a new desktop space

To add a new desktop space to Mission Control, click the **plus** button (**+**) in the top-right corner:

A new desktop space will then appear. You can open apps and folders within this space, and they will remain here, making it easy to start organising your apps and folders into multiple spaces.

Assign an app to a specific space

If you'd like an app to open in a specific space - rather than all of them - use Mission Control to visit the space you'd like to assign the app, right-click on its icon in the Dock, then choose **Options** > **This Desktop**.

Delete a desktop space

To delete a space, activate Mission Control, move the cursor over the space you wish to delete, then click the **close** (**x**) button:

Make the screen bigger or smaller

Change the size of everything on the screen to suit your needs...

When you first set up your MacBook, the desktop, folders, apps, text and icons are all sized at a comfortable level for someone with normal vision. The trouble is, not everyone has perfect eyesight, so those average-sized icons and sentences might be hard to see. Thankfully, there's a straightforward System Preferences panel for adjusting the size of *everything* on your Mac's screen. Here's how it works:

Adjust the screen size

1. Start by opening the **System Preferences** app, then click on **Displays**.

2. On the **Display** tab, click the **Scaled** radio button. You'll then see four options appear.

3. Try clicking on the different options to find a zoom level that's comfortable for you.

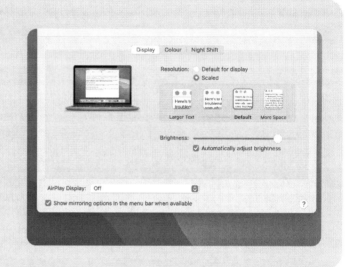

Make icons bigger or smaller

Every file and folder on your Mac is displayed using an icon that's 64 by 64 pixels in size. Basically, they're postage stamp sized. To make them bigger or smaller:

1. Go to the Finder or Desktop on your Mac, click **View** in the menu at the top of the screen, then choose **Show View Options**.

2. In the pop-up window, drag the **Icon Size** slider to the right to increase icon and folder sizes, or to the left to shrink them.

Toggle Dark and Light Mode

Enable Dark Mode, change colours, and more...

macOS has a beautiful, simple interface, but if you *really* look at it, you'll notice that it's mostly made up of white panels and windows. If you'd like to give your Mac a fresh coat of paint, then it's possible to enable Dark Mode, which gives all of those panels and windows an evocative dark appearance. Here's a comparison of the System Preferences app to give you with an idea:

How to toggle Dark Mode on or off

1 Open the System Preferences app. You'll find it in the Dock, but you can also find it by clicking the **Apple** logo at the top of the screen then **System Preferences**...

2 Click on **General**, then click on **Dark** in the Appearances section.

3 If you'd like Dark Mode to activate at nighttime, rather than all the time, then choose the **Auto** option.

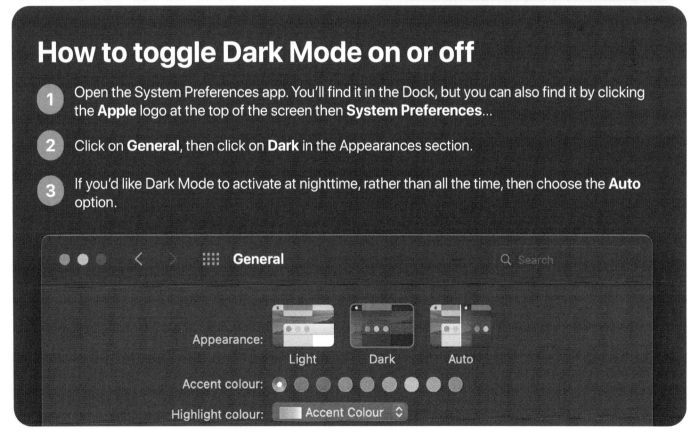

What is iCloud

Learn what iCloud is all about...

iCloud is a term used to describe a wide range of services, all of which are provided by Apple, and all accessed over the internet. Perhaps the biggest benefit of iCloud is that all of your photos, documents, music, apps, contacts, calendars and settings, are saved on the internet, and shared between all of your Apple devices. This means you can snap a photo on your iPhone then see it automatically appear on your Mac. It means you can purchase a song, movie or TV show, and see it appear on all of your devices. It also means you can start writing a document on your Mac, edit it on your iPhone and see the changes appear simultaneously across both devices. Here's a quick overview of some of the other features found within iCloud:

Photos

Any photo taken on your iPad or iPhone is wirelessly uploaded to iCloud, then automatically downloaded onto your other devices, Mac, or PC. So if you take a photo during the day on your iPhone, when you get home you'll see it waiting for you on our Mac, all without having to sync devices or use wires.

iCloud Drive

iCloud Drive automatically saves all your documents and desktop files. This means you can access them from another device, or a web browser via **www.icloud.com**. iCloud Drive also works with Pages, Numbers, and Keynote, so if you're writing a letter or creating a presentation on your Mac, you'll be able to continue editing it on your iPad or iPhone without having to worry about transferring the file. Edits are automatically updated across all of your devices.

Find My iPhone (for Mac)

If you can't find your iPhone, iPad, or Mac, the Find My iPhone feature in iCloud will enable you to locate it. By signing into your iCloud account, either from **www.icloud.com** or another iPhone, you can see all your devices on a map, set a passcode lock, remotely wipe them or send a message to the screen. You can also enable Lost Mode, whereby the device is automatically locked, a message with a contact appears on the screen, and the device automatically reports its location via iCloud.

Mac Backups

iCloud automatically backs up your Mac when it's plugged into a power source and connected to the web over Wi-Fi. iCloud backs up the following things: your desktop, folders and files, music, movies and TV shows, photos and videos, settings, app data and messages. If you buy a new Mac, then you can restore all of the above by using an existing iCloud backup.

Safari bookmarks and history

iCloud automatically saves your bookmarks, passwords, Reading Lists and open tabs. So if you begin reading a lengthy web article on your Mac, you can continue reading it at a later time on your iPad or iPhone.

Notes, accounts, reminders, and contacts

All of your notes, email accounts, reminders, and contacts are saved in iCloud, so whenever you make a change to these, it will be automatically sent to your other Apple devices.

iCloud Drive

Store all your files, settings, and media in the cloud...

Using iCloud Drive, you can store all your documents and desktop files in iCloud, then access them at any time using another device, such as your iPad, iPhone, or even a Windows computer using **www.icloud.com**. Not only does this make working across multiple devices easier, but it also means you have a backup of your entire Mac available, at any time.

Set up iCloud Drive

This part is easy. Just open the **System Preferences** app, select **iCloud**, then click **iCloud Drive**. The first time you enable iCloud Drive, you'll be asked to upgrade your iCloud account to support this feature. All this does is move any of your files from iCloud to iCloud Drive.

Once iCloud has been enabled, click the **Options**... button to the right of iCloud Drive, then click **Desktop & Documents Folders**.

Because you're storing your documents in iCloud, whenever you save a file or make a change, that file will be uploaded to iCloud using your network connection. Keep this in mind, because if you save a very large file to your Mac, it will be automatically uploaded to iCloud in the background and could, potentially, slow down your web connection.

Access iCloud Drive on your Mac

Whenever you want to access iCloud Drive using the Finder, open a new window then click the **iCloud Drive** shortcut in the sidebar.

Anything you to add to these folders is automatically synced via iCloud to all your devices. Similarly, if you delete anything, it is also deleted across all of your devices.

Access iCloud Drive on the web

Because iCloud works across the web, you can access your iCloud Drive from anywhere in the world using a desktop web browser. Just head over to **www.icloud.com**, sign in using your Apple ID, and click the **iCloud Drive** button.

To download a file, select it then click the **Download** button at the top of the screen (it looks like a cloud with an arrow pointing down). To download multiple files, hold down the **Command** key on your keyboard, select the files, then click the **Download** button.

Access iCloud Drive on your iPhone or iPad

If you own an iPhone or iPad, then you can also access iCloud Drive to view and save files from your Documents and Desktop folder. To do this open the **Files** app on your iPhone or iPad, tap **Browse** at the bottom of the screen, then **iCloud Drive**.

Safari tabs, bookmarks, and history

Enjoy a consistent experience across the web from device to device...

With iCloud enabled on your Mac, iPhone, and iPad, you can share the same browser history, bookmarks, and tabs across Safari on all of your devices. This means you can start reading a page on your Mac, then later pick it up on your iPhone.

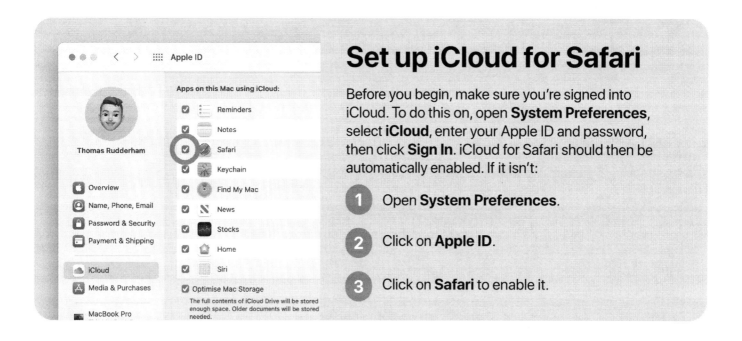

Set up iCloud for Safari

Before you begin, make sure you're signed into iCloud. To do this on, open **System Preferences**, select **iCloud**, enter your Apple ID and password, then click **Sign In**. iCloud for Safari should then be automatically enabled. If it isn't:

1. Open **System Preferences**.

2. Click on **Apple ID**.

3. Click on **Safari** to enable it.

How to use iCloud Tabs

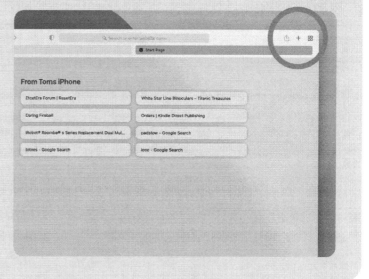

1. When you're using your Safari to browse the web, click the plus (+) button in the upper-right corner to open a new tab.

2. To see all the tabs open on your other Apple devices, simply screen the new tab downwards.

iCloud Bookmarks

Bookmarks are helpful shortcuts to all of your favorite websites. Using iCloud, these bookmarks will appear across all of your Apple devices, so you only need to add a bookmark once and it will appear within Safari on your Mac, iPhone, and iPad.

To see your iCloud bookmarks, open **Safari**, click the **Sidebar** button in the upper-left corner, then choose **Bookmarks**. Any bookmarks you have saved will then appear in the sidebar.

To add a new bookmark, visit the website you wish to add, then press **Command-D** on your keyboard. You can also click on **Bookmarks** in the top menu and choose **Add Bookmark**. A small menu will slide down the screen enabling you to enter a bookmark name and description.

To remove a bookmark, open the bookmark sidebar, find the bookmark you wish to remove, right-click on it, then choose **Delete**.

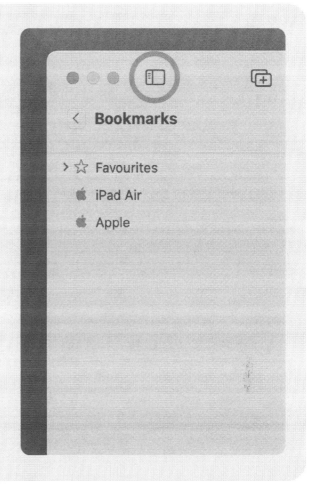

iCloud Browsing History

Whenever you visit a website in Safari, a log of that visit is stored in your browser's history, which you can access by pressing **Command-Y** on your keyboard.

With iCloud, your browsing history is stored across all of your Apple devices, so if you visit a website on your iPhone, then later open Safari on your Mac, you can see a log of that visit.

iCloud History is a helpful feature that makes browsing the web more seamless across all of your Apple devices, but if you would like to disable it:

1. Open **System Preferences**.

2. Click on **Apple ID**.

3. Untick **Safari** to disable iCloud History, Tabs, and Bookmarks.

Manage internet passwords

Reference, update, and delete your saved passwords...

As you browse the internet, you're likely to start registering for accounts across websites and cloud-based services. As you do, you'll be asked to enter personal details (such as your email address and telephone number), along with a unique password. Whenever you do this, Safari will automatically save your username, email address, and password, so the next time you visit the website you can login by using your fingerprint or Mac's password. These passwords are saved within Safari, and also automatically synced with any iPads, iPhones, and other Macs that you may own. If you later return to a website or service and update your password, it will automatically be saved and synced across all of your devices.

Access your saved passwords

1. Open **Safari** on your Mac, click on **Safari** in the Apple menu at the top of the screen, then click **Preferences**.

2. Click on the **Passwords** tab, then enter your Apple ID password or use your fingerprint to unlock the panel.

3. You'll then see a list of every website you've ever logged into.

4. You can search for a website, username, email address, or password, by using the search field at the top of the panel.

5. You can also click on individual accounts to see the details you've saved.

6. To delete a set of details, select it then click the **Remove** button at the bottom of the panel.

View or edit a password

Double-click on a username or password within the window and a small panel will appear. In this panel you can view and edit both the username and password.

Delete a password

Select a username and password from the list then click **Remove** at the bottom of the window.

Duplicate passwords

It's never a good idea to use the same password across multiple websites, especially if you use the same email address or username. While browsing the Passwords panel, you'll be warned of any duplicate passwords by a yellow triangle. If you see one, it's a good idea to visit the website associated with the password and then change it immediately. To look for duplicate passwords:

1. Click on **Safari** in the Apple menu, then choose **Preferences**.

2. Click on the **Passwords** tab. After entering your user account password, you'll see all the usernames and passwords saved within Safari.

3. Look for any yellow triangles next to passwords.

4. Click on a triangle, and you'll see a blue link, this will take you to the relevant website associated with the username and password. From there you'll be able to update the password and ensure it's unique to that website.

Basics of using the internet

A few things to keep in mind as you explore the internet...

Safari is the very best way to browse the web on your Mac. It's blazingly fast, rendering web pages in an instant. It supports Apple Pay, so you can make purchases on the web without entering your credit card details, it can strip all the ads and junk out of a page to show you only the content you want to see, it can automatically block pop-ups, and so much more.

Web addresses

Just like places in the real world, websites have addresses of their own. To visit a website, you'll need to enter its address into the bar at the top of the screen. Here's the address for Apple's website:

https://www.apple.com

First, there's the 'http', or 'https' part. The only thing you need to know about this is that the 's' stands for secure. This means your data is encrypted as it travels from your Mac to the website and back again, so no one else can see or access it. So whenever you visit a website that needs your personal information — like a bank or store — make sure there's an 's' at the end of 'https'.

Next is the 'www' part. This is short for 'World Wide Web', which is another term for the internet. You don't actually need to type this, as your browser will automatically fill it in for you.

Next is the actual address of the website, in this case, 'apple'. As you can see, this part of the address is typically the name of the company or person who owns and runs the website.

Finally, there's the '.com' part. This is called an extension and often hints at the location or type of website. '.com' websites are usually based in America, '.co.uk' websites are usually in the United Kingdom, and '.org' is usually an organisation that is primarily nonprofit.

Know what you're looking for

While the internet has billions of websites and pages to visit, most people only go to a handful of places on a day-to-day basis. Usually, it's their favourite news website, their favourite shop, and a social media website. That's possibly the best way to use the internet, because by sticking to a few regular websites, you can ensure that your data is safe and that the information you read is accurate. Which brings us onto the next point...

Don't believe everything you read

Anyone can post on the internet, so don't trust everything you see and read. Unlike traditional news websites, there's no fact-checker on social media websites such as Facebook and Twitter. This means anyone can post whatever is on their mind; whether it be their emotions, ideas, or even conspiracies. If something sounds suspicious, then it probably is.

Look for https when making a purchase

When making a purchase or entering personal information, make sure the website you're visiting is protected by https security. There's an easy way to check: just look for a grey padlock icon in the address bar at the top of the window.

Use Safari to browse the web

Visit websites, organise tabs, customise your experience, and more...

Safari is the very best way to browse the web on your Mac. It's blazingly fast, rendering web pages in an instant. It supports Apple Pay, so you can make purchases on the web without entering your credit card details, it can strip all the ads and junk out of a page to show you only the content you want to see, it can automatically block pop-ups and so much more.

The basics

1   Click the **sidebar** button to access your tab groups (see across page), open a Private tab, see content shared with you, access your bookmarks, reading list, and browsing history.

2   Use these arrows to go back a page, or forward a page.

3   Click on the **address bar** to enter a website's address, or to search Google.

4   Click this **curved arrow** to refresh the page.

5   Click the **Share** button to send a webpage to someone else, message a link, email a link, print the page and much more.

6   Click this button to see an overview of all the tabs and windows open in Safari.

7   This light grey bar indicates the active tab.

8   You can open a new tab tab by clicking this button (see across page for more on tabs).

Visit a website

Open Safari for the first time and you'll see a blank canvas. To visit a website, just click on the **address bar** at the top of the screen, then enter its web address; for example, www.apple.com.

Search the web

The address bar in Safari also acts as a search engine, so to search the web for any question or search term, just type your query into the address bar at the top of the screen.

Use tabs to visit more than one website

Think of a tab as a single view of a webpage. You can have as many tabs open on your Mac as you like, but you can only view one at a time. To open a new tab view, click the **plus (+)** button in the top corner.

Explore and close tabs

To see an overview of all your tabs, click the **tabs** button in the very top corner of the screen. To close a tab, click the small **X** button in it's top-left corner.

If you accidentally closed a tab and want to go back to it, click and hold the **plus** button (**+**) and after a second a pop-up window will appear showing your recently closed tabs.

Create a group of tabs

If you have many tabs open on your Mac, then it might be a good idea to group them into categories. By doing this, you could create a tab group for home, a tab group for work, and a tab group for everything else.

To create a group of tabs, click the **sidebar** button, then click the **new tab group** button in the upper right corner. To create a new tab group from scratch, click **New Empty Tab Group**. Alternatively, you can create a tab group using all the tabs currently open by clicking **New Tab Group from (number) Tabs**. After making a choice, enter a name for the tab group, then click **Save**.

Jump between tab groups

To jump to another group of tabs, click the **dropdown arrow** next to the tab button, then make a choice. You can also click the **sidebar** button and then select a group from the panel.

Add a page to a tab group

If you're in one group of tabs, and wish to save a page to another group of tabs, **right click** on the **page tab** at the top of the screen, select **Move to Tab Group**, then make a choice.

Delete a tab group

To delete a group of tabs, click the **sidebar** button, right click on the group you would like to delete, then choose **Delete**.

Add a bookmark

If you visit a website regularly then it's a good idea to bookmark it. This lets you easily re-visit the website by either opening a new tab, or by clicking the **sidebar** button and then **Bookmarks**. To add a new bookmark, click the **Share** button at the top of the screen, then choose **Add Bookmark**.

Manage your bookmarks

To quickly visit your bookmarks, click the **sidebar** button, then choose **Bookmarks**.

To remove or edit a Bookmark, right click on it and then choose **Delete**.

Add a favourite

Whenever you click on the address bar or open a new tab, Safari will display your favourite websites. This is a helpful way to access your frequently visited sites without having to type their URL each time.

To add a new favourite, click the **share** button and choose **Add to Bookmarks**. You can then choose between bookmarks and favourites using the dropdown menu.

To delete a favourite link, click the **sidebar** button, choose **Bookmarks**, expand the **Favourites** list, then right click on the favourite and choose **Delete**.

Use multiple windows

If you'd like to view two websites at once, then press **Command-N** on your keyboard, or go to **File > New Window** in the Finder menu.

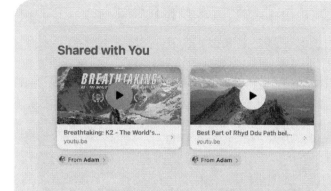

See content shared with you

If someone has shared a link with you via the Messages or AirDrop, then you can always find it at a later date by clicking the new tab button (**+**). then scrolling down, where you'll find a **Shared with You** panel.

Use Safari Reader to remove clutter

Often, when you visit a website, it can be hard to focus on the content of a page because of distracting adverts, images, and layout. Safari has a great feature called Safari Reader, which removes all the clutter from a web page to leave you with just the content you came to see. To enable Safari Reader, load a web page, then click the **Safari Reader** button within the address bar.

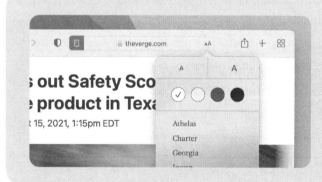

Customise Safari Reader

While using Safari Reader, it's possible to tweak the font, background colour, and text size. To do this just click the **aA** icon in the address bar.

Edit saved credit card details

The first time you enter credit card details into Safari, it will ask you if you would like to save the card details on your Mac. Agree to this, and the credit card number, expiry date, and account name will be saved. The 3-digit code on the back will not be saved for security purposes. By saving these details, the next time you try to buy something Safari will auto-fill your card's details, saving you considerable time.

If you would like to edit any saved credit card details, click on **Safari** in the Apple menu at the top of the screen, choose **Preferences**, then click **AutoFill**. On the following panel, look for **Credit Cards** and then click the **Edit** button. You can then click on each credit card field to make changes. To delete a credit card, select it and then click the **Remove** button.

Simplify the tab bar

Default view, with tabs below address bar

By default, tabs open on your Mac appear below the address bar at the top of the screen. This makes it easy to distinguish the address bar from the tabs, but it takes up a lot of space at the top of the screen.

You can simplify this by merging the address bar with tabs, resulting in a cleaner look which gives the page below more room to show content. To this click on **Safari** in the Apple menu at the top of the screen, choose **Preferences**, then click **Tabs**. On the following panel, choose the **Compact** option, and you'll see both the tabs and address bar merge into one.

Compact view, with tabs and address bar merged.

Check your email

Compose messages, organise your inbox, and more...

Having your own email address is pretty much a requirement for using the web today. You need an email address to register website accounts, make purchases, and receive messages... basically any productive task involved with using the web. Thankfully, the Mail app in macOS is brilliant, and it's designed with a clean interface that helps you focus on what's important: your emails.

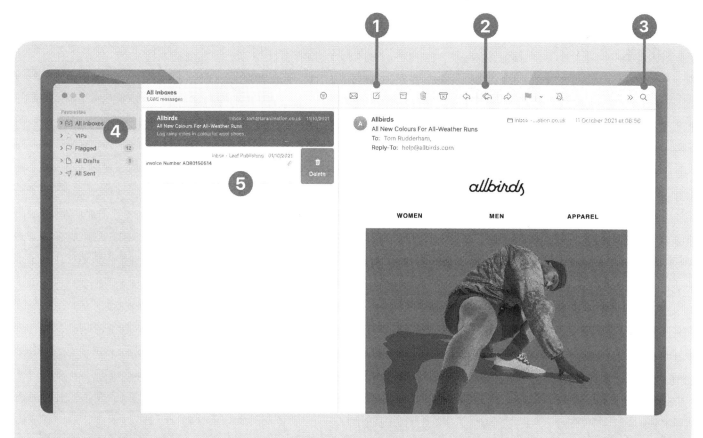

The basics

1 Create a new email by clicking this button in the upper-left corner of the screen.

2 These shortcut buttons enable you to delete an email, reply, forward, flag, archive, or move an email to another folder.

3 Click on the **Search** button to (you guessed it) search through your emails. You can look for people, email content, dates, or attachments.

4 You can navigate through multiple accounts and folders using the sidebar.

5 Move the cursor over an email, then swipe horizontally with two fingers across the trackpad or Magic Mouse. Swipe towards the left and you'll be able to delete the email in an instant. Swipe towards the right and you'll be able to mark it as Unread.

Send an email

When you're ready to send an email, click the **new email** button at the top of the screen, or press **Command-N** on the keyboard. You'll then see the compose window pop into view. Here's an overview of what each field does:

- **To**: In the field, type the email address of the person or organisation that you wish to email.
- **Cc**: In this field, enter the email addresses of people that you want to include, but are not addressing directly.
- **Subject**: Type a short title to describe your email.

In the large space below, type your email. When you're ready to send it, click the **grey arrow** in the top-left corner.

Format text

To format text within an email, click the **Format** button at the top of the message window (**Aa**), then use the controls to format your text. It's possible to change the font, size, colour, alignment, style, indentation, and background colour.

Attach an image

There are a couple of ways to attach an image with an email:

1 Click the **photo** button in the top-right corner, then either choose a photo from your library, or take on using your iPhone or iPad.

2 Drag a photo from the desktop or a folder onto the email window.

Save a draft email

While composing an email, click the **close** button (or press **Command-W** on the keyboard) and Mail will ask if you would like to save the message as a draft. You can find all your draft emails in the sidebar on the left.

Add an attachment

To add an attachment, click the **Attach** button at the top of the message window (it looks like a paperclip), then choose the file on your Mac. You can also drag and drop attachments onto the mail draft window.

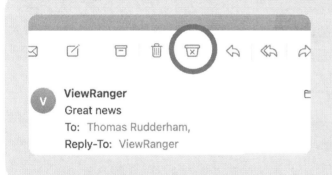

Mark a message as spam

If you've received an email that you didn't expect or sign-up for, then select it and hit the **Spam** button at the top of the Mail window. Any similar messages from the same recipient will automatically be moved to the Spam mailbox.

Embed a web link

To embed a web link into a piece of text, highlight the text, **right-click**, then choose **Link > Add Link**. In the pop-up field, enter the link URL, then click **OK**.

Send an email to multiple recipients

While composing a new email, enter the recipients address into the To: field. To add a second person, either click the blue plus (**+**) button, or use a comma to separate addresses.

Delete multiple emails at once

To delete more than one email at once, hold down the **Command** key, then click on the emails you wish to remove. Once you've selected them all, press the **delete** button.

Save a contact

To save a contact's email address to your Mac, hover the cursor over their name at the top of the email, click the small arrow which appears then choose **Add to Contacts**.

Include an emoji

Sending an emoji to someone is a fun way to add humour to an email. To explore and add an emoji:

1 Click the **Emoji** button in the top-right corner of the email draft window.

2 Explore the emojis by scrolling through the pop-up window, or use the search field to find an exact match.

3 Double-click on the emoji you want to use, and it will be inserted into the email.

Chat using Messages

Send messages, photos, videos, emojis and more...

If you haven't already guessed, the Messages app is for sending messages, photos, emojis, and even audio messages to friends and family. It works best if you have an iPhone, as the app can use it to send and recieve regular text messages; but even without one you can still message anyone else with an Apple device, such as another Mac, iPhone, or iPad.

The basics

1. Use the search bar to look for people, keywords, or attachments.

2. To begin a new conversation with someone, just click the **New** button in the upper-left corner.

3. Click on the **FaceTime** button to start a phone or video call, mute someone or see any shared attachments.

4. Click on the **info** button to see more information about a contact, the content they've shared, and any contact links.

5. You can right-click on a conversation to delete it, mute the person, or open the chat in a separate window.

6. Swipe across a conversation (using either the trackpad or Magic Mouse) to mute alerts or delete it.

Send a message

To send your very first message:

1 Click the **new message** button in the top-right corner of the sidebar.

2 In the **To**: field, start typing the name of someone in your Contacts book, or the phone number of someone you know.

3 Enter your message in the iMessage field at the bottom of the window, then press the **Enter** key to send the message.

Adjust text size

If you're struggling to read the text within a conversation, click on **View** in the menu, then select **Make Text Bigger**. You can keep adjusting text until it's large enough, or revert it back to its default size

Audio messages

Sending an audio message to someone is both quicker than typing, and also being more personal. To do this, click on the **audio** button in the bottom-right corner, then start talking out loud. When you've finished saying your message, click the red **stop** button; then to send the audio message, click the blue **arrow** button.

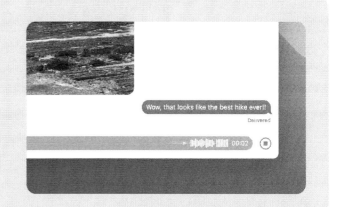

Delete a conversation

There are a few ways to remove a chat conversation:

- **Swipe right-to-left** across the chat conversation in the sidebar.
- **Right-click** on the conversation in the sidebar, then click **Delete Conversation...**
- Select the conversation in the sidebar, click **File** in the menu at the top of the screen, then choose **Delete Conversation...**

Pin conversations

If you chat to someone on a regular basis, then it's a good idea to pin their conversation to the top of the sidebar. That way you can quickly find them without having to search or scroll through the sidebar. To pin someone:

- **Swipe left-to-right** across the chat conversation in the sidebar, then click the yellow pin button.
- **Right-click** on the conversation in the sidebar, then click **Pin.**

Send an emoji

To send a regular emoji, click on the grey **Emoji** button next in the bottom-right corner. A pop-up window will appear, letting you scroll vertically through a massive number of emojis.

If there's a specific emoji that you're looking for, try using the search field at the top of the pop-up window to find it.

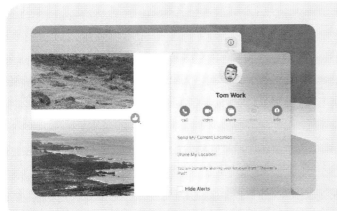

See more about a conversation

While viewing a conversation, click the **Info (i)** button in the top-right corner. In the pop-up window you'll be able to call or email the person, share your location, hide any more alerts, and see media attachments.

Send a photo or video

To send a photo with a message, click the **App (A)** button and choose **Photos**. In the pop-up window, select a photo from your library, then double-click to send it.

Send a full-screen effect

To really surprise someone, compose a message, click the **App (A)** button, then choose **Message Effects**. You can then choose from a number of full-screen effects.

Block someone

Click on their conversation, then click **Conversations** > **Block Person...** To manage blocked contacts, open the **Preferences** window, and go to **iMessage** > **Blocked**.

Make a FaceTime video call

Make a free video call to friends and family using FaceTime...

Using the FaceTime app, you can make a video call to anyone you know that has an iPhone, iPad or Mac. As a result, you can be with friends and family at any time and any place; whether it's a birthday, anniversary, meeting, or just a quick chat.

FaceTime works over the internet, so as long as you're connected then you're good to go. Once you make or answer a call, you'll be able to enjoy crystal clear video and audio, and perhaps best of all, it's totally free to use the FaceTime app.

The basics

1 Take a photo of the conversation using this button. The other person will see a message to let them you've captured an image.

2 Click on the **sidebar** button during a call to invite other people to the call.

3 Mute your microphone.

4 Flip your video from portrait to landscape, or vice versa.

5 Turn of your video camera during a call.

6 End the call by clicking on the red **X** button.

7 Click this button to blur the background behind you. It's a helpful way to bring the focus to yourself, rather than what's behind.

Make a regular phone call

Yes, you can use your Mac as a giant telephone. It works by routing the call through your iPhone in the background without you knowing. To do this:

1 Select a contact using the list on the left-side of the screen, or click the **plus** button then type a contacts name.

2 You can also type a phone number, then press the **enter** key.

3 Click the **Audio** button. Your Mac will then dial the number and make the call.

4 To end the call, just click the red button.

Change the ringtone

If you would like to personalise your FaceTime experience with a new ringtone:

1 Click on **FaceTime** in the Finder menu bar and select **Preferences**.

2 Click the **Ringtone** drop-down, then choose a new ringtone. When you select one you'll hear a preview of it through your Mac's speakers.

Block people

If you're getting a lot of spam calls then it's possible to block people using either their email address or number. To do this:

1 Click on **FaceTime** in the Finder menu bar and select **Preferences**.

2 Click on the **Blocked** tab.

3 Click the **plus** button in the bottom left corner then enter the email addresses or phone number you wish to block.

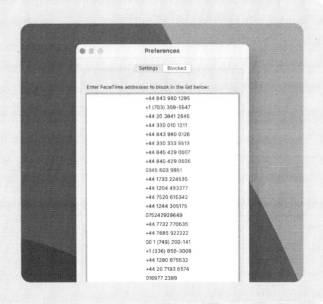

Take a selfie with Photo Booth

You can even apply up to 30 different visual effects...

Want to quickly take a selfie? The Photo Booth app on your Mac is the perfect way to snap a photo or even record a brief video. You can also choose from more than 30 visual effects which include mirror warp and moving imagery.

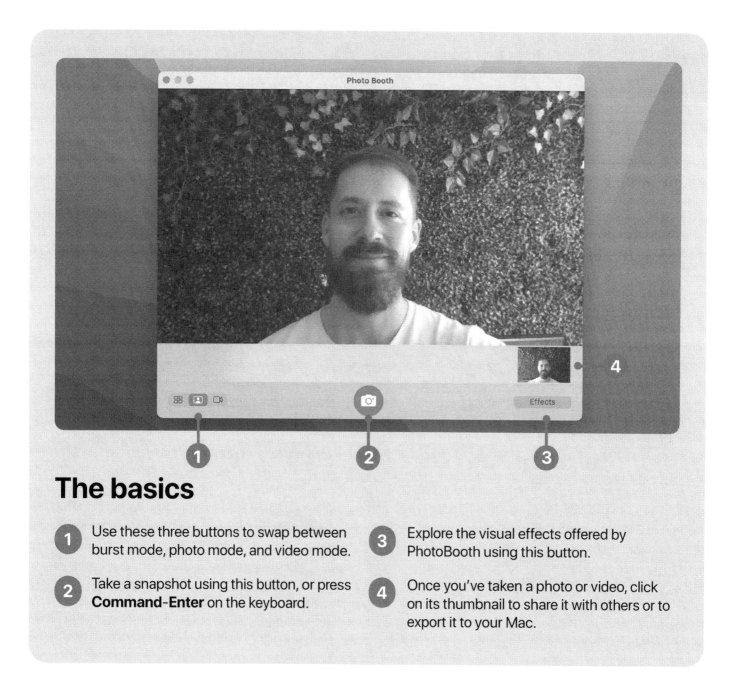

The basics

1 Use these three buttons to swap between burst mode, photo mode, and video mode.

2 Take a snapshot using this button, or press **Command-Enter** on the keyboard.

3 Explore the visual effects offered by PhotoBooth using this button.

4 Once you've taken a photo or video, click on its thumbnail to share it with others or to export it to your Mac.

Check your Stocks

Monitor the latest stocks and news, straight from your Mac...

Whether you're keeping an eye on the latest stocks, betting against them, or monitoring your portfolio, the Stocks app for macOS is a helpful way to quickly get updates on stocks and news.

Open the Stocks app, and the first thing you'll see is a sidebar listing the leading 10 stocks. To its right are the latest stock-related news stories.

The basics

1 To add a new stock, click on the **Search** field at the top of the sidebar, then search for either the company name or its stock name.

2 Click on an individual stock and you'll see a graph of its latest performance.

3 To rearrange the Stocks in the sidebar, **click and hold** on a stock, then drag it up or down to its new position.

4 Click on a stock and you'll see any relevant news stories here.

View and edit your Photos

Learn how to view, organise, and edit your photos...

The Photos app is a portal to your memories. Stored within its colourful icon are hundreds, if not thousands of treasured photos and videos. Photos of yapping dogs, family members, stunning landscapes, unflattering selfies and treasured holidays. This is one of those apps that you're going to be opening on a day-to-day basis, so keep it somewhere prominent on the Dock where you can quickly click it.

The basics

1 Use the slider to zoom in and out of your photos.

2 Click these 4 tabbed buttons to see your entire photo library split across days, months and years. See across the page for more.

3 Click on a photo, then click the **info (i)** button to see more information about an image, such as the device it was captured with, and the location whaere it was taken.

4 Select **Search** to look for nearly anything in a photo, including both people and objects.

5 The sidebar enables you to navigate through your albums, tagged people, places, favorites, deleted images and more.

An overview of the date categories:

All Photos

When viewing **All Photos**, you'll see a nearly endless grid of photos scrolling upwards and off the screen. You can scroll through them and click on an image to see it bigger, or you can use the slider in the top-left corner to see your photos spread over a wider range of time.

Days

Click on the **Days** tab and you'll see a beautiful grid of images representing a single day. The Photos app intelligently organises your images, hiding duplicates while selecting a highlighted image or video.

Months

The **Months** view organises the most meaningful events into groups, then displays them as individual cards in a scrollable panel. The app tries to intelligently select the best photo or video to remind you of what the event was about. Think of it as a greatest hit library of your memories.

Years

Years gives you a high-level overview of your photo library, but what makes this view really special is it's dynamic and based on context. So open the Years view on your birthday and you'll see photos from your birthday celebrations going back as far as your photo library extends.

Search through photos

The Photos app is incredibly intelligent. Using complex visual algorithms it can recognise objects, faces, and locations, then automatically organise images into groups. This clever form of visual recognition has another benefit: intelligent searching. It lets you search for things within an image by typing a request. To find this feature, simple click the **Search** button in the top-right corner.

Search for "*California*" and you'll see all your photos of California. Search for "*Trees*" and you'll see (you guessed it) images of trees. You can be even more specific. So search for "*Trees in California*" and the Photos app will automatically show photos of trees within California. You can try other queries such as "*Tom eating pizza*", or "*Sarah riding a horse*" and the app will instantly present you with the correct results.

Find People and Places

After scanning every photo in your library to look for photos of locations and faces, the Photos app collates them into the **People and Places** section of the Photos app.

To see these images, open the Photos app, then click either **People** or **Places** in the sidebar.

Add a name to a person

To add a name to someone in the People album, move the cursor over their thumbnail then click the **+ Name** button.

Favorite someone

If you like to regularly see the photos of a family member or friend, click on the **heart** icon to move them to the favorites area at the top of the screen.

Share a photo or video

Open an image, then click the **Share** icon in the top-right corner of the screen – it looks like a box with an arrow pointing upwards.

Select multiple images

To select multiple photos at once, click and drag the cursor over the images you wish to select. You can also hold down the **Command** key then click on multiple photos.

How to delete a photo

The easiest way is to **right-click** on the image, then choose **Delete Photo** in the pop-up window.

The basics of editing a photo

To improve the look of a photo, click the **Edit** button in the top-right corner, and a set of editing tools will appear:

1. Toggle between adjustment tools, filters, and the cropping tool using these tabs.

2. Rotate a photo 90 degrees using this small button at the top of the screen.

3. Click on an editing tool to access its controls. Here you can see individual sliders for adjusting the light balance of an image.

4. You can change the key image of a Live Photo by scrubbing through this timeline.

Automatically improve an image

To automatically improve an image, click the **Wand** icon at the top of the screen. This tool analyses the image and changes its colour, contrast, and lighting to improve it.

Crop an image

While editing a photo, click the **Crop** tab, then either drag the edges of the image to crop it, or choose a ratio option from the sidebar on the right.

Rotate a photo

While cropping a photo, you can also rotate it. To do this, click and drag the rotate wheel to the right of the image. As it rotates you'll see a grid appear that enables you to align straight edges or an horizon.

Add a filter

The middle tab at the top of the screen enables you to add a visual filter to your image. You'll find nine to choose from, each with its own unique appearance.

Remove small objects or blemishes

Photos are rarely perfect. There might be an object spoiling the view, a shadow you wish to remove, or a spot that you need to paint out. The Photos app makes it easy to fix these small errors or objects. Click **Edit**, expand the **Retouch** tool, then click on the brush icon. Next, click on the object or blemish, and the Photos app will attempt to automatically remove it.

111

Fix red eyes

If you used a flash while taking a photo, then anyone within the image might have red pupils. To fix this, click **Edit**, expand the **Red-Eye** tool, click the small brush button, then click on each red eye in the photo.

See information about a photo

Whenever you're viewing or editing a photo, click the **info (i)** button at the top of the screen to view technical information and location-based data.

Create an album

It's possible to create your very own albums to better organise your photos. To do this:

1 Hover the cursor over **My Albums** in the sidebar, then click the **Plus** button.

2 Give your album a new name.

3 Click on **Photos** at the top of the screen, right-click on an image then choose **Add To > New Album**.

4 You can also click and drag photos into the new album in the sidebar.

Move images between albums

You can move images between albums by right-clicking on them then choosing **Add To** > **New Album**. You can also drag them from one album to another in the sidebar.

Merge albums

If you'd like to merge two albums into one, then click and drag an album in the sidebar on top of another. A pop-up window will appear asking you to confirm the merger of both albums.

Delete an album

It's easy to delete albums from your Mac. Just **right click** on them in the sidebar then choose **Delete Album**.

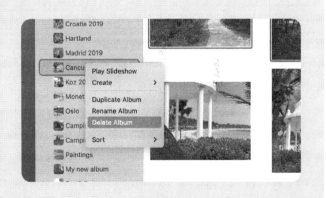

Listen to Music

Listen to your favourite tracks and albums on Apple Music...

The Music app is best way to listen to music on your Mac. It has a beautiful interface, offers access to millions of tracks via Apple Music, exclusive TV shows, curated playlists, videos, top charts, and even radio stations.

There's a limitless source of music available in Apple Music, but it comes at a price: to access the full service you'll need to pay a monthly subscription. It's priced slightly differently for each country, but roughly works out about the same as a takeaway pizza. For anyone who listens to the latest charts, streams music on a daily basis, or has a wide variety of music tastes, it's definitely worth the asking price. If you don't want to pay a subscription to listen to music, then you can still use Apple Music to listen to radio stations and preview music.

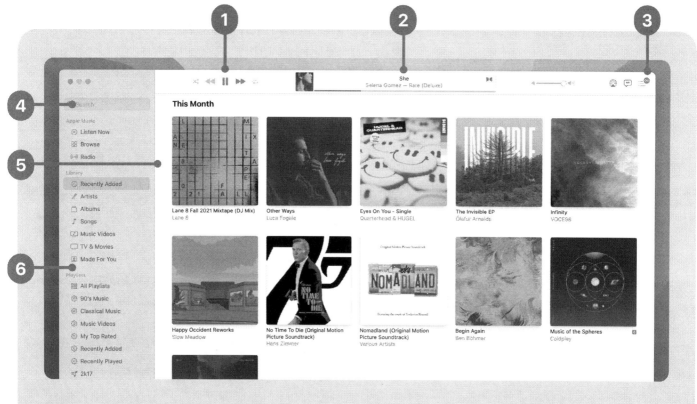

The basics

1 Shuffle, rewind, pause, fast forward, and loop music playback with these buttons.

2 Scrub through a song using this timeline. By clicking on the artwork thumbnail you can also minimise the Music window.

3 Click on this icon to display a right-hand sidebar with all the upcoming tracks.

4 Search both your music library and Apple Music for artists, songs and albums.

5 Click on an album to explore it, or right-click to delete it, share it, or Love/Dislike it.

6 Use this sidebar to navigate through Apple Music, your library, and any saved playlists.

Apple Music

Apple Music is a monthly subscription to nearly every music track and album ever released. Without an Apple Music subscription, the Music app is severely limited, offering only 30-second previews that stream over the internet.

You can sign up for a monthly subscription through the Music app by clicking either **Listen Now** or **Browse** in the sidebar.

Search for music

If you're looking for an artist, song, album, or even lyrics, then click the **Search** bar in the sidebar. You can use the two tabs in the top-right corner to search through either Apple Music or your library.

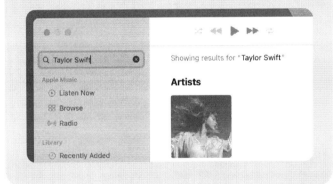

Add music to your library

If there's a track or album that you'd like to save to your Library, click the **+Add** button at the top of the screen.

View music lyrics

Have you ever struggled to understand the lyrics of a song as it plays in the background? Using the Music app you can see lyrics for all your favourite songs, and they update in realtime so you can follow along. Think of it as your own karaoke machine. Here's how it works:

When listening to a song, click on the **lyrics** button in the top-right corner of the screen. It looks like a small speech bubble. You'll then see a lyrics sidebar appear on the right-side of the screen.

Shuffle music

If you're bored of an albums track order, click **Shuffle** and you'll never know what song is coming up next.

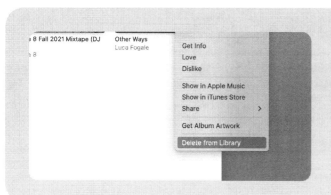

Delete a track or album

Fed up with a song or album? Just **right-click** on the track name or album artwork, then click **Delete from Library**.

Display the Mini Player

The Music app takes up a lot of space across the screen, but helpfully there's a miniature version that's easier to manage. To display it:

1 Click on **Window** in the Apple menu at the top of the screen, then click **Mini Player**.

2 You can now minimise the main window by pressing **Command-M**.

3 To close the Mini Player, click the **red button** in the top-left corner.

Create a station

If you're listening to an album or track and want to listen to similar music, then your Mac can automatically look for similar tracks and albums, then turn them into an endless radio station. Here's how it works:

1 While listening to music, click on the **options** button at the top of the screen.

2 Click on **Create Station**. Your Mac will then start playing an endless stream of similar music.

Create a Playlist

Think of a playlist as a custom-made album. To create a playlist of your own, click on **File** in the menu, choose **New**, then **Playlist**. You can then give it a name.

Add music to a playlist

To add a track or album to the new playlist, **right-click** on the track then choose **Add to a Playlist...**

Listen to the radio

Click **Radio** in the sidebar to listen to Apple Music 1, radio stations from around the country, or bespoke stations that are automatically compiled around your listening history.

See the top charts

Want to see what's number one in the charts? Click on **Browse** in the sidebar, scroll down to the bottom of the screen, then click **Top Charts**.

Read books

Explore, buy, and read books on your Mac...

The Apple Books app is the single destination for all the books you love, and the ones you're about to. Open the Books app on your Mac, and you'll be able to browse the Book Store, keep track of what you've read and want to read, and listen to enthralling audiobooks. All in one place. Here's an overview of what you'll find when you open it for the first time:

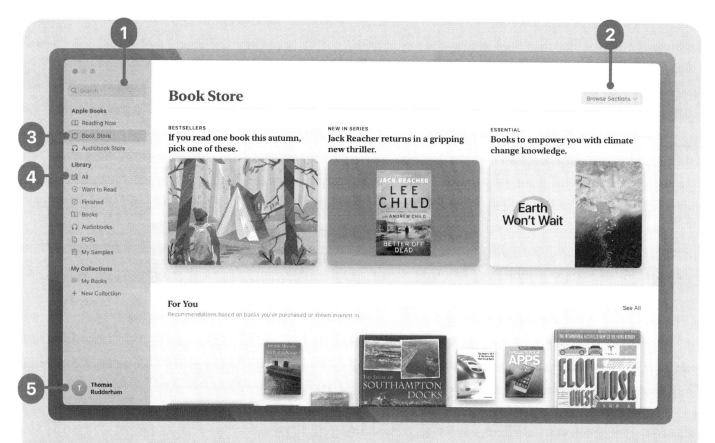

The basics

1 If you already have a book in mind, use this search field to find it in the Books store.

2 Use this menu to explore genres, top sellers, award-winning books, and titles with the highest ratings.

3 These three links enable you to continue reading a book, explore the Books store (as seen in this image), and explore the Audiobooks store.

4 These links in the sidebar enable you to jump between your books, audiobooks, PDFs, and sample books.

5 Click on your username in the bottom corner to adjust settings, redeem a gift card, explore your purchases, and sign out.

Read books

Double-click on a book in your library to open it and start reading. If you close the book, the app will remember where you were and take you back to the same page when you re-open it.

View the table of contents

To jump between the chapters of a book, move the cursor over it while reading, then click the **Table of Contents** button in the upper-left corner.

Adjust text size

To change the text size and font style of a book, move the cursor over it while reading, then click the **Aa** button in the top-right corner.

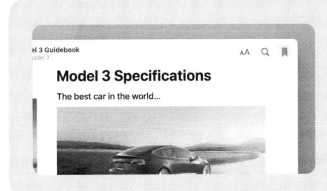

Add a bookmark

While reading a book, click the **bookmarks** button in the top-right corner and you'll bookmark the page. You can view all the bookmarks and jump to each one by clicking the small downward-facing arrow, just to the right of the bookmark button.

Watch TV & Movies

Never miss an episode of your favorite show with this helpful app...

With so many sources of video content, subscription services, and streaming neworks, it has become difficult to keep track of the latest episodes of your favorite TV shows. Thankfully, the Apple TV app for the Mac makes it a little bit easier, by collating many of the latest releases into one app. It also houses any TV shows or movies which you've purchased on iTunes, enables you to stream videos to your Apple TV, and remembers where you last left off.

The basics

1 If you're looking for inspiration, click **Watch Now** to find suggested TV shows and movies.

2 Click the **Kids** tab to find a wide range of content suitable for children.

3 It's pretty obvious, but by clicking **Search** you can look for movies, TV shows, or cast.

4 Explore the very latest film rentals and purchases by clicking on **Movies**.

5 You'll find all of your purchases in the **Library** section of the app, split into TV Shows and Movies.

6 Quickly jump between suggested movies, TV, or kids shows with these helpful shortcuts.

Toggle audio and subtitles

While watching a video, click the **speech** icon next to the playback timer to toggle different audio sources or subtitles.

Access special features

If you've rented or purchased a movie with special features, then you can access these by clicking the **Extras** button in the bottom-right corner of the screen.

Jump between chapters

Click on the **Chapters** button in the bottom-right corner to skip through a movie. You can also move the cursor to the top of the screen and use the Chapters menu option too.

Find out more about cast

Search for an actor, producer, director, or other member of crew, and you can see what films they've been in, created, or made a guest appearance.

Watch videos with QuickTime

A helpful tool for watching and trimming local video files on your Mac...

Installed on your Mac is a helpful little app called QuickTime Player. It's the default player for videos you might download from the internet, but it can also be used to play audio files, crop videos, or record your Mac's display in its entirety.

Play a video

Double-click on a video file and it will open in QuickTime Player. Press the **spacebar** key to begin playing the video, or move the cursor over it to access controls which enable you to play, pause, adjust the volume, scrub along the timeline and share the video.

Fast forward or rewind

Hover over a video to access its controls, then click on the **forward/back arrows** and you'll play the video back at double-speed. If you triple-click the arrows you'll play the video back at 5x speed, click 4 times for 10x playback speed.

Go frame-by-frame

If you want to study a video in detail, simply press the **left** or **right** arrow keys on your keyboard and you'll be able to scrub through the video one frame at a time. Hold down an arrow key and the video will play back at half speed.

Watch a video full screen

If you really want to settle down and enjoy a video, press **Command-F** to play it back full screen. You can also go to **View** > **Enter Full Screen** to perform the same command.

Resize the video window

If you want to adjust the size of the video playback window simply move your cursor to the corner of the video, then click and drag it. You'll see the video window change in size as it follows the cursor.

Trim a video

You might not know it, but QuickTime Player supports basic video editing tools, enabling you to trim a video then re-save it in various formats. Here's how it works:

1. While viewing a video, press **Command-T** to access the trim tools.

2. Drag the yellow handles to trim the video to its new length.

3. Click the **Trim** button to save your changes.

Use Maps to explore the world

Discover new places, get route guidance, and more...

With a map of the entire globe on your Mac, it's now possible to explore every inch of the world. That's exactly what the Maps app gives you, alongside directions, real-time traffic information, transit timetables, 3D views of major cities and more.

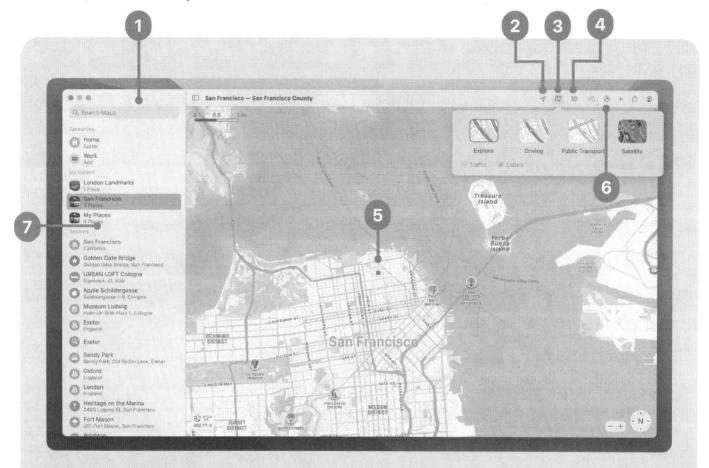

The basics

1 Click on the **search field** to search for a place, address, or landmark.

2 Click on this **arrow** icon to move the maps view to your current location.

3 Click on the **view** button to choose from three different views of the world: Default, Public Transport, and Satellite.

4 Click the **3D** button to tilt the camera upwards slightly.

5 This blue dot represents your current location in the world.

6 Click the **directions** button to get route guidance from one location to another.

7 The sidebar automatically displays your recent activity. You'll also find any collections of places you've saved alongside recently viewed locations.

Swap view modes

When you open the Maps app, you'll see the world in a 2D vector mode. If you'd like to view satellite imagery instead, click tap the **view** button at the top of the screen, then choose **Satellite** in the panel which appears.

View live traffic

If you're planning a road trip, then it's a good idea to see how busy the route ahead is. To see live traffic on the map, click the **views** button at the top of the screen, then click the small **Traffic** button. You will then see coloured lines appear on the road to indicate traffic. Green represents flowing traffic, orange means slow, while red means very slow.

Explore what's nearby

To find local businesses and places of interest, click on the **search** field at the top of the screen, then use the various icons to see what's nearby. Scroll down, and you'll also find articles and guides to nearby cities.

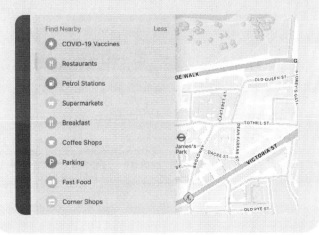

FaceTime a business or find out more

If you're exploring the map and find a local business or place of interest, click on it to find out more. You might see TripAdvisor reviews, photos, opening times, phone numbers, and useful pieces of information.

See a 3D map

Using the Maps app it's possible to navigate the world's most famous cities in beautiful 3D graphics. To do this, ensure you're in **satellite** mode then zoom in on the map. When you're close to the ground, you'll notice a **3D** button appear in the upper-right corner. Click it and the Maps view will tilt, then load a 3D landscape with detailed 3D buildings.

- To rotate the image, place two fingers on the trackpad then rotate them, or hold down the **option** key then move the mouse left or right.
- To tilt the camera, simultaneously move two fingers up or down the trackpad, or hold down the **option** key and move the mouse up or down.

Look Around in first-person

Chances are you've seen Google's Street View. It's a great piece of technology that lets you explore the world at street level using 360-degree imagery. Apple's Look Around mode is similar, but it's more polished, realistic, and includes tags that you can click on to explore businesses and landmarks.

To use the Look Around mode, zoom the map until you see a binocular icon appear in the top-right corner. At the time of writing, it will only appear in major cities within the United States. Once you see it, click the **binocular** icon, and the map view will zoom down to street level.

- To pan the view, click and drag the cursor around the screen. To move in any direction, double-click where you want to go. You can also click on a tag to see more information about the place or business.
- One last tip: click the **minimise** icon in the top-left corner to shrink the Look Around view and place it above the 2D map. You can now click on a new location on the map, and the Look Around view will update to show you street-level imagery.

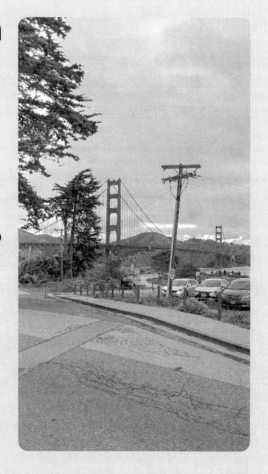

Drop a pin to find out more

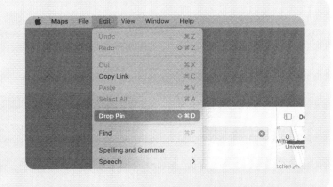

To see detailed information about a specific point, zoom into that spot, click Edit in the Apple menu, then choose Drop Pin. A pin will then fall on the map and display information about the location.

Search indoor maps

With the Maps app you can find your way around airports and shopping centres using the indoor maps feature, which displays the locations of stores, toilets, and more. Most international airports and major shopping centres are fully mapped. Just look for a "Look Inside" badge that appears beneath the name of the airport. When you see it, click **Look Inside**.

Share a location

Want to send an address to friends and family? Just search for the location then click the **Share** icon in the top corner of the screen.

Get walking or cycling directions

If you're planning a route on foot or a bike, then use the small graphical buttons to select either walking or cycling directions. If going by bike, then you can plan a route that avoids hills and busy roads.

Search Maps using Siri

If you'd rather search for a place using Siri, click the **Siri** icon in the Finder menu or press the **Siri** button on the TouchBar then say something like *"where is the nearest hotel?"*.

Add a scale to the map

If you need a better idea of distances and scale, click **View** in the Finder menu then select **Show Scale**. In the upper-left corner of the map you will now see a scale (in either km or miles).

Turn-by-turn navigation

Your Mac can't be used as a sat-nav device, but it can plan directions for you and offer multiple routes.

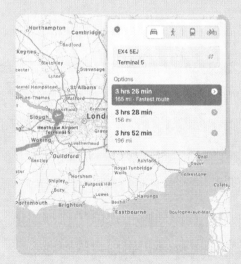

1 Open Maps then click the **Search** field at the top of the window. Next, enter the destination you wish the navigate too. This can be an address, post/zip code, or landmark.

2 Once you've searched for an address a pop-up window will appear showing details for the location. Click the blue **Directions** button, and Maps will automatically find the optimal route to the destination. It will also offer alternative routes, if any are available, which appear as opaque blue lines on the map.

3 Once you've found a suitable route tap, click the **small arrow** button in the directions suggestions panel, and you'll see an overview of the entire journey.

Enjoy a flyover tour

Want to explore a city like never before? Simply search for the city's name then click the **Flyover Tour** button in the information panel. You will then be treated to a 3D tour of the city.

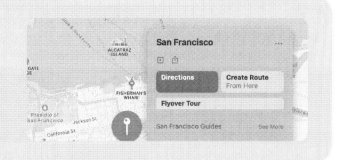

Report an issue with the map

To report an error or missing place, click **Maps** in the Apple menu, then choose **Report an Issue...**

Create Reminders

Set yourself reminders so you'll never forget a thing...

Your Mac includes a notes app that can be used to jot down ideas and thoughts, but Reminders makes it easy to create to-do lists, set deadlines, and organise your life. It can also remind you with alerts at pre-determined times.

That's not all the app does, of course. It can group reminders into categories and even sync reminders across all your Apple devices via iCloud.

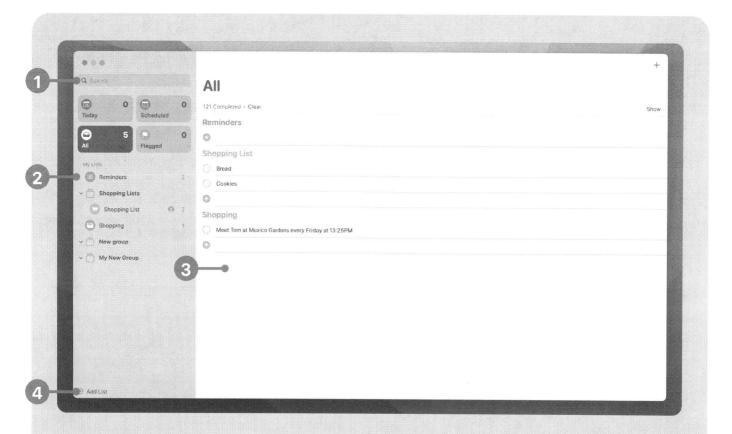

The basics

1 Search for reminders, lists, or list items using the search bar at the top of the screen.

2 Select a reminder or list here. You can also rearrange items by clicking, holding, then dragging.

3 You can add additional items to a reminder list by clicking in the white space beneath an item.

4 To create a brand new reminder list, click the **Add List** button in the bottom-left corner.

Create a new Reminder

Click the **Reminders** option in the sidebar, then click the **Plus** icon in the very top-right corner. This will create a new reminder in the main panel.

Date and time reminder

To remind yourself to do something at a specific date and time, click on the new reminder, then click the **i** button. On the next panel, click **Remind me on a day**, then set a day and specific time if necessary.

Set a location reminder

Similarly, you can also remind yourself when you reach a location. To do this click the **Remind me at a location** button, then either enter an address or choose from one of the suggested options.

Create a folder

You can create folders of reminders by dragging one on top of the other in the sidebar. You'll then be able to give the new folder a name.

Create a reminder using Siri

You can also add reminders by using Siri. Just click the **Siri** icon in the top corner of the Finder menu, then say something like *"Remind me to pick up Sam"*. Siri will then automatically create a new reminder.

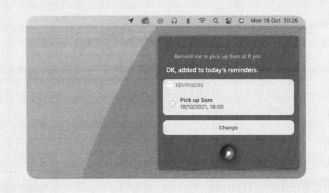

Create, edit, and share Notes

Learn how to quickly jot down notes, plus much more...

At first glance, the Notes app is a fairly basic way to jot down ideas and lists. It's much more than that, however. With the Notes app you can collaborate with friends, draw and annotate, scan documents, format text, create tables and more.

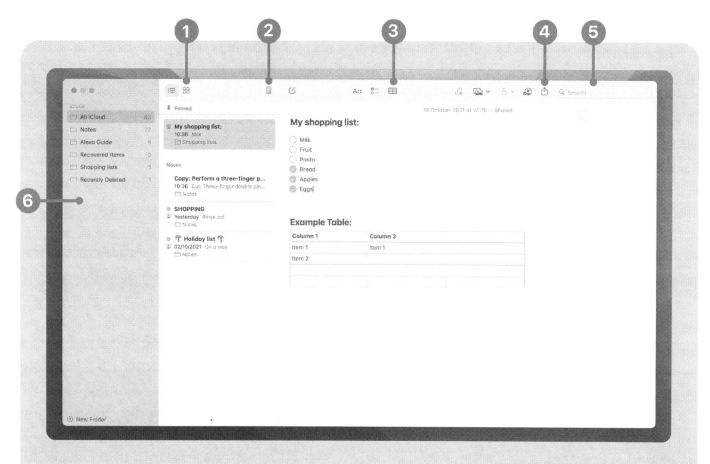

The basics

1 You can view your notes as thumbnail images (rather than a list view) by clicking this icon.

2 To delete a note, select it first then click this **Trash** icon.

3 Create a table within a note by clicking this icon.

4 Share, print, or save a note by clicking the **Share** button.

5 Search through your notes by entering a keyword into the search field.

6 You can jump between different Note accounts and folders by using this sidebar.

Create a new note

To create a new Note, open the **Notes** app then click the **New Note** button in the upper-left corner. You can also press **Command-N** on the keyboard.

Sketch in a note

You can use your iPhone or iPad to add a sketch into a note. To do this click the **Photo** button at the top of the screen, choose **Add Sketch**, then select your iPhone or iPad.

While drawing a sketch on your iPhone or iPad, you can change the colour of the line by tapping one of the coloured dots along the bottom of the screen. Tap on the multicoloured circle to access additional colours.

Insert a photo

Click the **Photo** button at the top of the screen, then choose **Photos...** You can also drag and drop an image from the Finder onto the note.

Add bulleted lists

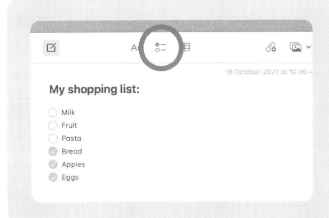

If you're making a list of items (such as a shopping list), then you can create bulleted lists and check them off one by one.

To do this, write the first item on the list, then click the **tick** button at the top of the Notes app. To add a second item press the **return** key. To mark items as complete, click the **circle** to the left of the item.

Scan a document

If you have an iPhone to hand, then it's possible to scan letters and documents and attach them directly to a note on your Mac. What's great is that scans actually look like scanned documents, thanks to some clever post-processing which straightens the image and fixes any white balance issues. To scan a document:

1 Start by clicking the photos button in the top corner, then choose **Scan Documents**.

2 The camera on your iPhone will automatically open.

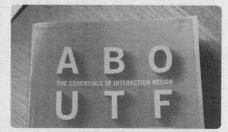

3 Move the camera view over the document you wish to scan and your iPhone will automatically recognise it.

4 Tap **Keep Scan** to save the image. You can continue to scan further documents, or tap **Save** to attach the image/s to your notes.

5 The scan will now be attached to your note as an image.

Change the default text size

If you find the default text size too small (or too big), then click **File** in the Finder Menu, choose **Preferences**, then use the **Default text size** slider to adjust text size.

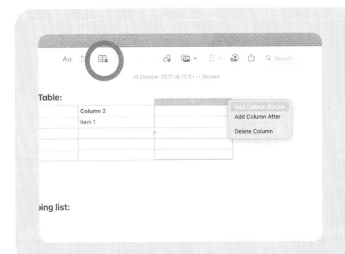

Create a table

Start by creating or opening a note, click where you want to insert the table, then click the **Table** button at the top of the screen.

You can add content to a row or column by clicking the appropriate area, or add additional rows and columns by clicking the buttons above or to the left of the table.

Format text

To format text or add a numbered/bulleted list, click the small **Aa** button at the top of the screen, then choose an option.

Share a note

Want to send a note to someone else? Just click the **Share** button and you'll see options for emailing the note, sending it to another device via AirDrop, or copying it.

Delete a note

While viewing the notes list, swipe across the note you wish to remove from right to left, or right-click and choose **Delete**.

System Preferences overview

Get to know the basics of the System Preferences app...

Whenever you want to make a change to your Mac, adjust a setting, or add a new piece of hardware, then System Preferences is the place to go. You can access System Preferences at any time by:

- Clicking the **Apple** logo in the Finder menu, then **System Preferences**.
- Clicking the **System Preferences** icon in the Dock.
- Opening the **Launchpad**, then clicking **System Preferences**.

Once you open the System Preferences app you'll see a grid of shortcut icons. They're labelled logically, so if you want to add another user account to your Mac, then click Users & Groups; and if you want to change the background wallpaper choose Desktop & Screen Saver.

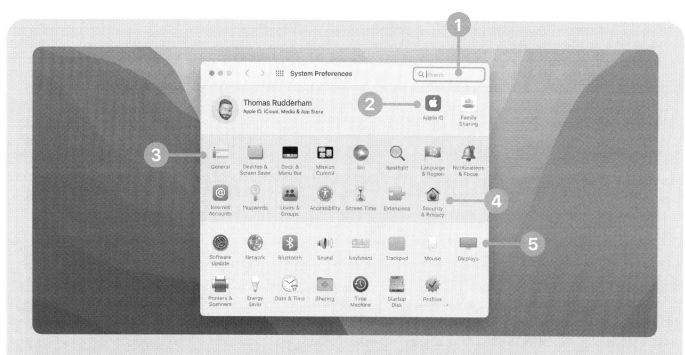

The basics

1 If there's a particular setting that you're trying to find, use the **search** field to quickly locate it.

2 Click **Apple ID** to edit your personal details, password and security settings, and iCloud settings.

3 Click on **General** to toggle Dark Mode on or off, or adjust the basic colour scheme.

4 You can change your password, open apps from outside of the App Store, and access an entire suite of privacy settings from here.

5 Adjust the brightness, resolution, colour profile, and Night Shift settings from here.

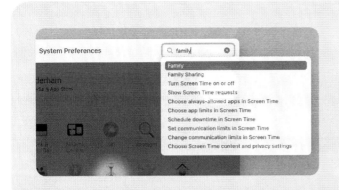

Search through Settings

If you're not sure where a particular setting is, then you can quickly search for it using the **Search** box in the top-right corner. As you type, System Preferences will attempt to guess what you're looking for, then use a spotlight to show you where to go.

Explore Battery panel

It's a good idea to put it your Mac to sleep whenever you're not using it, but if you prefer to leave it on all the time, or adjust how your Mac manages efficiency while running on battery power, open the **System Preferences app**, click **Battery**, then click the **Battery** option in the sidebar.

Adjust the date, time, or temperature format

To quickly toggle between locations, date and time formats, temperature formats, and calendar formats, open **System Preferences** and click on the **Language & Region** option in the upper-right.

Enable voice dictation

If you'd like to talk to your Mac to dictate text, open **System Preferences**, select **Keyboard**, then click the **Dictation** tab. You'll then see an option to turn voice dictation on and use it wherever you type text.

Users & Groups

Learn how to create separate accounts for those who use your Mac...

If your Mac is the main computer at home, then it's likely that at some point another member of your household is going to use it. Maybe they want to quickly print something, or perhaps they want to use it to work for a few hours; whatever the reason, it's probably a good idea to set up a separate account for them.

By creating separate user accounts, you can let each person personalise settings, save their own passwords, install apps, and modify options without affecting anyone else. You can also create groups of users to share privileges between multiple people.

Add a new user

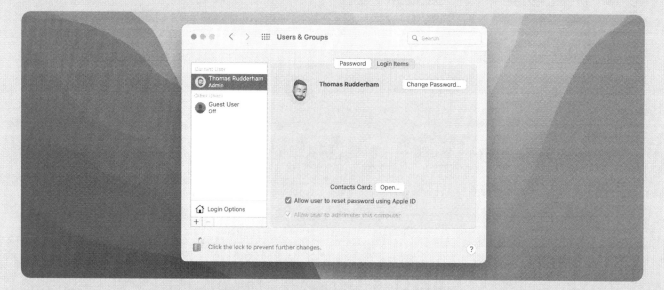

1. Open the **System Preferences** app, then click on **Users & Groups**.

2. Click the **padlock** icon, and enter the administrator username and password.

3. Click the **plus** button underneath the list of users.

4. In the New Account pop-up menu, choose a type of user. Here's a quick overview of each:
   - **Administrator**: An administrator can add and manage other users on your Mac, install new apps, and change any setting.
   - **Standard**: Standard users can also install new apps and change their own settings, but can't add other users.
   - **Sharing Only**: The most limited type of account, Sharing Only users can only see files shared to the Mac remotely, and can't change settings on the Mac.

Automatically log in

If you don't want to enter your password every time you turn on your Mac, then it's possible to skip the login screen entirely. This saves time, but it's worth noting that anyone who turns on your Mac can also log in and access your files. If you're sure that no one else will ever have access to your Mac, then:

1 From **Users & Groups**, click the **Login Options** button underneath the list of users.

2 Click on the **Automatic Login** dropdown, then select the appropriate user from the dropdown list.

Add a new group

By creating a group of users, you can easily share privileges between multiple people. For example, you can create a rule that lets a group of users share access to the same folder, or limit a group from installing any third-party apps. Here's how it works:

1 From **Users & Groups**, click the **Add** button underneath the list of users.

2 In the **New Account** pop-up menu, select **Group**.

3 Give the group a name, then click **Create Group**.

4 A new window will appear, enabling you to assign users to the new Group.

Create a guest account

By creating a guest account you can have a separate account for relatives and friends. This prevents anyone using your Mac from seeing your files and settings, and you can assign limitations to guest accounts to prevent people from doing things that they shouldn't. To activate the guest account:

1 From **Users & Groups**, click on the **Guest User** account.

2 Click the checkbox next to **Allow guest to log into the computer**.

Family Sharing

Let the entire family share media, purchases, and even games...

With Family Sharing enabled on your Mac, it's possible for up to six family members to share content and purchases across iTunes, Apple Music, Apple Books, the App Store, Apple News+, and Apple TV. One adult in the household needs to act as the administrator. They can invite other family members, choose features, and approve purchases; while the rest of the family enjoys shared music, photos and more.

Basic features:

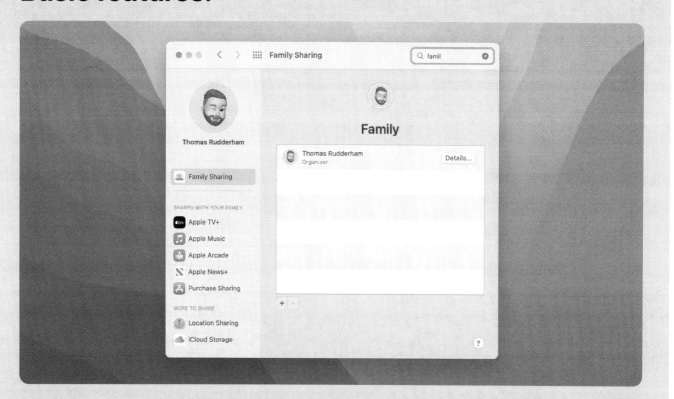

- **Share purchases.** Once an app, TV show, movie or book is purchased, it's instantly available to everyone else too.
- **Apple Music.** Unlimited music for the entire family with a family membership plan.
- **iCloud storage.** One plan to store everyone's photos, files, and backups.
- **Location Sharing.** Everyone in the family can share their location via the Messages app or Find My Friends. They can also track each other's devices.
- **Apple TV content.** The whole family can access the latest Apple TV shows across their devices.
- **Apple Arcade subscription.** Let everyone in the family play the latest games in Apple Arcade.
- **Apple News+.** Get the latest magazines and exclusive news stories.

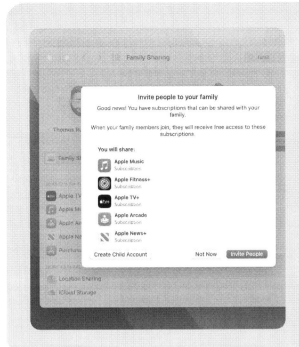

Set up Family Sharing

The adult in the family is the one who should set up Family Sharing. If they enable purchase sharing, then they will be asked to verify that they agree to pay for purchases initiated by family members. With that in mind, the next step is to:

1 Open **System Preferences**, then click on **Family Sharing**.

2 Follow the on-screen prompts to enable Family Sharing. You'll be asked whether you'd like to share music, movies, TV shows, apps and books purchased with your Apple ID. You'll also be asked if you'd like to pay for purchases made by other members of your family.

Invite a family member

Whenever you want to add a family member:

1 Open **System Preferences**, then click on **Family Sharing**, then click **Add family member....**

2 Enter your family member's name, email address, or Game Centre nickname.

If they're with you they can enter their Apple ID address and password and be added straight away. Otherwise, an invitation will be sent on your behalf.

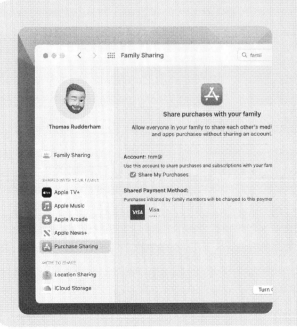

Enable Purchase Sharing

With Purchase Sharing enabled, you can buy something from iTunes, iBooks, or the App Store, then everyone in your family can download it for free too. To turn Purchase Sharing on:

1 Open **System Preferences**, then click on **Family Sharing**.

2 Click **Purchase Sharing** in the sidebar.

3 Click the **My Apps & Services** tab.

4 Click the **Share my purchases** checkbox.

Restrict content

Make sure your kids don't access anything inappropriate...

Letting your kid's roam free on the internet is a scary idea. Thankfully, you don't have to look over their shoulder all the time, because the Content Privacy Restrictions panel in Screen Time lets you protect them while they browse the web. It's possible to block adult websites, explicit content, set time limits, and monitor what they can access.

Turn on Content & Privacy Restrictions

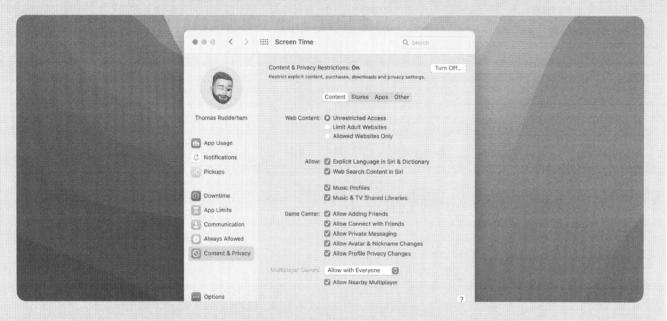

To restrict content, you'll first need a separate user account for your kid's. Once created, you can begin setting restrictions and time limits. Here's how it works:

1. Log into the account you wish to restrict, then open **System Preferences**.

2. Next, click on **Screen Time**. Look for the **Content & Privacy** option at the bottom of the sidebar. Click it, then click **Turn On...** in the upper-right corner.

3. Most of the options are fairly self explanatory, so to restrict adult websites, click **Limit Adult Websites**.

4. To create a custom list of approved websites, click **Allowed Websites Only**, then click **Customise...** to add and edit a pre-populated list of child-friendly websites.

5. Click the **Apps** tab and you can prevent children from opening built-in apps, enabling the camera, or using Siri.

6. Click the **Other** tab and you'll find options for preventing a child from making passcode changes, account changes, and even using mobile data.

View an activity report of your Mac usage

Using the Screen Time panel it's possible to view daily or weekly reports of your Mac usage. You can see how long you've spent using apps, how many notifications you've received, and even how many times you've opened apps (Apple calls this "Pickups").

1 Open the **System Preferences** app, then click on **Screen Time.** At the top of the panel you'll see a brief report on how long you've spent using apps.

2 Click the **Categories** button below the graph and you'll see a brief overview of the total time spent on your Mac, broken down into categories.

3 To see how long you've spent using apps over the course of a week, click on the date in the upper-right corner, then choose **This Week**.

4 Click on **Notifications** in the sidebar to see which apps have been sending you the most notifications.

5 Click **Pickups** in the sidebar, and you'll see how many times you've opened apps.

Other things you can restrict using Screen Time

By navigating through the sidebar in the Screen Time panel, you'll find options for limiting apps, or blocking a massive amount of content and features, including:

- App installation
- Location Sharing
- Changes to passcodes
- Account changes
- Mobile data limits

- Volume limit
- Explicit language
- Screen recording
- Multiplayer games
- Explicit entertainment and books

143

Security

Keep your data, apps, and personal details secure...

Your Mac contains personal information, treasured photos, contact details, payment details, messages, and more, so it's incredibly important to protect it with the right types and levels of security.

The basics

The first place you should visit is the **Security & Privacy** panel in the **System Preferences** app. Once there you'll see four tab shortcuts for accessing the following security settings: General, FileVault, Firewall, and Privacy. To make any changes, click the **padlock** icon in the bottom-left corner, then enter your account password.

Change your password

Click the **Change Password** button within the **General** panel. In the slide-down panel, enter your old password, your new password, then a subtle password hint.

Privacy Settings

The **Privacy** tab in the Security & Privacy panel lets you monitor and control a number of different settings:

- **Location Services.** From here you can prevent apps and services from accessing your location.

- **Contacts, Calendar and Reminders.** From these three panels you can prevent apps from accessing your personal data.

- **Photos.** Click on this panel to see which apps have requested access to your photo library.

- **Accessibility.** You can't control accessibility settings from here. Instead, you can see which apps are able to control your Mac using accessibility features.

- **Analytics.** From this panel you can share data with Apple and app developers, such as how you use their apps or any crash log data.

Require a password after putting the Mac to sleep

By default, your Mac will ask for your password immediately after it has gone to sleep, or after the screen saver begins. To change this from anywhere between five seconds and eight hours, look for the **Require password** drop-down, then use it to select a period of time.

Turn on the Firewall

A Firewall works by constantly monitoring your Mac's network connection, then blocking any unwanted traffic coming in or out of your machine. It's a good idea to have it running all the time to ensure your Mac stays safe from potential threats. To do this:

1. Click the **Firewall** tab within the **Security & Privacy** panel, then click the **padlock** icon in the lower-left corner and enter your account password.

2. Click **Turn On Firewall.**

3. Click the **Firewall Options** button and, in the dialog box that appears, click the **Enable Stealth Mode** checkbox. This will make your Mac invisible on public networks, such as a shared Wi-Fi connection within a hotel.

Keep in mind that a Firewall will only protect you from threats on the web. It can't prevent local attacks, which typically happens when a rogue app is installed locally on your Mac.

A guide to accessibility settings

Enable visual, audio, and physical accommodations...

Your Mac might be an intuitive computer to use, but it's also packed with assistive features to help those with visual impairments or motor control limitations. You'll find the majority of them in the Accessibility panel within the System Preferences app. To get there, open **System Preferences**, then select **Accessibility**.

Quickly access options

By default, you can access common accessibility options at any time by quickly pressing the Touch ID button three times.

From this panel you can quickly turn on accessibility features such as Voice Over, Sticky Keys, and Screen Zoom. Alternatively, to add an accessibility shortcut to the menu:

1. Open the **System Preferences** app.

2. Select **Accessibility**.

3. Click **Show Accessibility status in menu bar.**

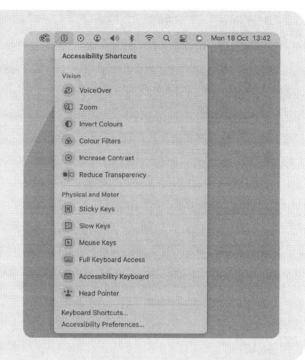

Make the cursor bigger

If you're struggling to see the cursor there are two things you can do. First, try shaking the mouse or shaking your finger on the trackpad. You'll see the cursor jiggle and get bigger for a moment. Second, you can actually make the cursor bigger. To do this:

1. Open the **System Preferences** app, then click **Accessibility**.

2. Click **Display** in the sidebar, click the **Cursor** tab, then use the **Cursor size** slider to increase the cursor size.

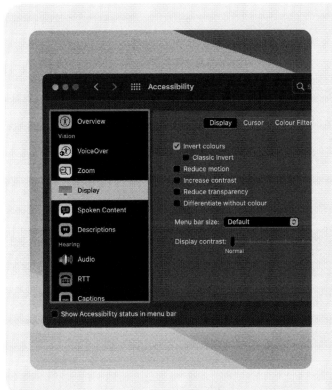

Invert the colours of your screen

For those with a sensitivity to brightness, macOS includes an accessibility feature that inverts every colour of the screen. Cleverly, media content like photos and videos *are not* inverted. To turn it on:

1 Open the **System Preferences** app, then click **Accessibility**.

2 Click **Display** in the sidebar, then click **Invert colours.**

3 You'll instantly see your Mac's screen invert. If you don't find this option helpful, then you can deactivate it by clicking **Invert colours** once again.

Zoom the screen

There might be occasions where you need to zoom the entire screen. Perhaps the text on a website is too small, or you can't quite make out the detail on an image. Thankfully, using a keyboard shortcut it's easy to zoom in and out:

1 Open the **System Preferences** app, select **Accessibility**, then click **Zoom** in the sidebar.

2 Click **Use keyboard shortcuts to zoom**.

To zoom in, press **Option** > **Command** > **=** on your keyboard. To zoom out, press **Option** > **Command** > **-**

To pan the screen, simply move the cursor to the edge of the screen and it will follow the cursor.

macOS Updates

Make sure you've always got the latest system updates installed...

Keeping your Mac up to date with the latest software releases is the best way to prevent security threats, fix software bugs, and get access to the latest features. Your Mac will always remind you when there are updates available via a notification alert in the top-right corner of the screen, but it's easy to manually check for updates, or schedule updates to install when you're away from the computer.

Check for system updates

To check whether a software update is available for your Mac:

1 Open the **System Preferences** app, then click **Software Update** in the lower-left corner.

2 Your Mac will check with Apple to see if any updates are available.

3 If so, then you'll see the version number and a brief summary. To install the update, click **Update Now**.

Check for app updates

If you're looking to update the apps on your Mac, rather than the operating system, then you'll need to visit the App Store instead:

1 Open the **App Store**.

2 Select **Updates** in the sidebar.

3 Either update individual apps, or click **Update All** in the top-right corner.

Manage user passwords

If you've forgotten your Mac's password, don't worry...

It's not always easy to remember your passwords, especially if you've been sensible and used unique passwords for all of your devices and accounts. If you ever forget the password for your Mac, then it's possible to reset it over the internet, so long as you remember the login details for your Apple account (also known as your Apple ID). If so...

Reset your Mac's login password

1. Start by restarting your Mac. To do this click on the **Apple** logo in the top-left corner, then choose **Restart**.

2. After your Mac restarts, click on your user account, click the **question mark** in the password field, then click the **arrow** next to **reset it using your Apple ID**.

3. Enter your Apple ID and password, then click **Next**.

4. Follow the instructions to reset your login password.

Reset the password of another user

If you're the administrator for your Mac, then you can reset the password of other users.

1. Start by restarting your Mac. To do this click on the **Apple** logo in the top-left corner, then choose **System Preferences**.

2. Click the **Users & Groups** option, then click the **padlock** in the bottom-left corner.

3. Select a user in the sidebar, then click **Reset Password**.

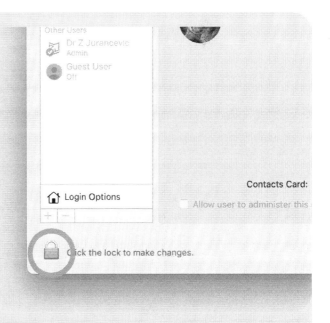

Use your iPad as a second screen

Use Sidecar to extend or mirror your desktop onto an iPad...

If you have an iPad released in 2018 or later, then you can use it to extend or mirror your Mac's display. There's no app to install, and everything works wirelessly (although you can plug your iPad into your Mac to keep its battery topped up). Apple calls this feature Sidecar, and it works by extending your Mac's display to one side. Think of it as extra screen space for you to place things. You can also mirror your Mac's display if needed, plus it's possible to use an Apple Pencil to tap and edit things that are placed on the iPad display.

Extend or mirror your Mac desktop

1. Click the **AirPlay** icon in the Apple menu, then select your iPad. If you don't see the AirPlay icon, then open **System Preferences**, click **Sidecar**, then use the **Connect to** dropdown to select your iPad.

2. Your iPad should now show an extended part of your desktop. You can drag windows onto it and use it like a second monitor.

3. Another way to move windows (and apps) to the iPad is to hover the cursor over on the green fullscreen button in the top-left corner of a window/app, then choose **Move to my iPad**. The window or app will instantly appear on the iPad and be perfectly formatted to fit its display.

4. To mirror your Mac's screen, rather than extend it, click on the **AirPlay** icon in the Apple menu (which now looks like a blue rectangle), and choose **Mirror**.

5. To finish extending your desktop, click on the **AirPlay** icon and choose **Disconnect**. Alternatively, you can tap the **Disconnect** button on your iPad's display.

Sidebar controls

Take a look at the sidebar on your iPad and you'll see a number of controls running down the side of the screen. Here's what each button means:

Tap this to show or hide the menu bar when viewing a window full screen.

This will show or hide the Mac's Dock on the iPad.

Touch and hold to set the **Command** key. Double-tap to lock the key.

Touch and hold to set the **Option** key. Double-tap to lock the key.

Touch and hold to set the **Control** key. Double-tap to lock the key.

Touch and hold to set the **Shift** key. Double-tap to lock the key.

Undo the last action. Some apps will support multiple undos.

Display an on-screen keyboard.

Disconnect your iPad from the Mac.

Display a Touch Bar on the iPad

The MacBook Pro comes with a built-in Touch Bar for acessing shortcuts throughout both the desktop and apps. You can also display this Touch Bar on your iPad:

1. Open **System Preferences**, then click **Sidecar**.

2. Tick **Show Touch Bar**, then use the drop-down menu to choose a location on the iPad's screen.

Use an Apple Pencil to edit things

If you have an Apple Pencil with your iPad, then you can use it to draw, edit photos, sign documents, and manipulate objects. You can also use your Apple Pencil as a replacement for the mouse or trackpad to select things.

Use a monitor as a second screen

Give yourself some extra space to work with...

Plugging a monitor into your MacBook is actually a pretty good idea, because by using a second display it's possible to extend your desktop, mirror it and get a larger view, or run two fullscreen apps at once. Here's how to set up and use a second screen with your Mac...

Get started with a second monitor

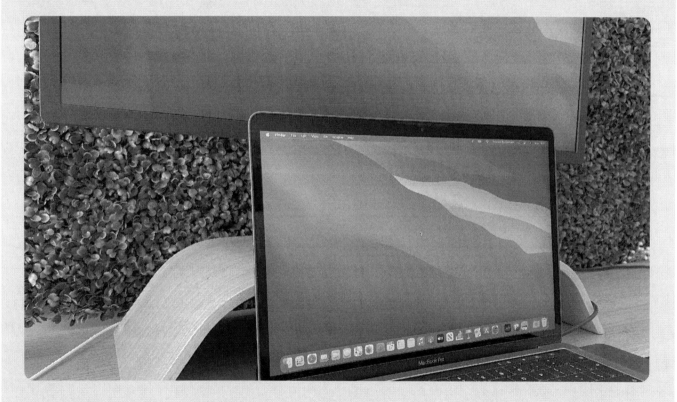

1. Before you plug any screen into your Mac, check what ports it offers. Ideally, you should get a monitor with a Thunderbolt port, because this enables your Mac to send data to the monitor while also being powered by it. You also won't need an adapter.

2. If you have a monitor with Thunderbolt support, simply plug one end of a Thunderbolt cable into the monitor, then the other end into your Mac. It will instantly power up and connect.

3. You can also use a HDMI cable to connect your Mac to a monitor. These are the same types of cables used for your TV, and are readily available from most electronic retailers.

Change the arrangement of your displays

If you're extending the desktop across both displays, and you want to drag files, folders, and windows from one screen to another, then you need to have them arranged properly in System Preferences. To do this:

1 Open **System Preferences** then click **Displays**.

2 Click on the **Arrangement** tab. You'll see a simplified graphic of the two displays. To work out which one is which, click and hold on a monitor. A red border will then appear around both the graphic and the monitor.

3 To move the new monitor to the left, right, above, or below your MacBook display, simply drag the new monitor and place it in the correct position.

Move the Dock and menu bar between monitors

When you work with multiple displays, one will need to act as the 'main' display and show the Dock and menu bar. To set the main monitor:

1 Open **System Preferences** then click **Displays**.

2 Click **Arrangement**. Look for the white bar running along the top of a monitor graphic. This represents the main display.

3 To change the main display, click and hold on the white bar, then drag it to the other monitor.

Mirror the displays

If you'd like to mirror your MacBook screen onto the monitor, then open **System Preferences**, click **Displays**, click **Arrangement**, then click **Mirror Displays**.

Extend your Mac's battery life

Keep the battery going for a little longer with these helpful tips...

The battery within your MacBook is intended to last all day on one charge, which is pretty impressive when you consider the amount of technology packed within it. However, if you're planning to spend a lot of time away from a plug socket, then there are some clever ways to try and extend your MacBook's battery life.

Before we get to that, it's important to note that all batteries used in electronic devices such as your MacBook lose their ability to hold a full charge over time. This isn't a cynical ploy to encourage you to upgrade to a new device, but rather a result of the current technology used in batteries worldwide. Each time a battery discharges 85% of its capacity, then re-charges to 100%, is considered one charge cycle. It is suggested that every MacBook will lose 20% of its battery capacity after 1,000 charge cycles. That means if you re-charge your Mac every day you can expect to lose half the original battery capacity after 2-3 years. If you leave it plugged in most of the time, then it will last a lot longer.

With that out of the way, let's take a look at some of this things you can do to extend your MacBook's battery:

Dim the display

The screen of your MacBook is one of the biggest drains of battery, so lower its brightness to extend the length of time you can run without a source of power. To adjust the brightness, you can either use the brightness slider on the Touch Bar, or via the **Displays** panel in **System Preferences**.

See if any apps are using energy

If you suspect an app is using lots of battery, just click the **battery** icon in the Apple menu at the top of the screen. Any apps using significant energy to run will be listed in the drop-down menu.

Disable Power Nap

Your Mac will periodically check for new emails, calendar events, and other iCloud updates, even even it's asleep. Admittedly this doesn't use a significant amount of energy, but if you'd like to save a small amount of battery life, then open **System Preferences**, click on **Battery** in the sidebar, then untick **Enable Power Nap while on battery power**.

Enable automatic graphics card switching

If you have the 16-inch MacBook Pro, then your machine actually comes with two graphics cards. One for powering the Mac for day-to-day tasks like browsing the web, and another for powerful graphics-related tasks like rendering video and playing games. By default, your Mac will switch between the two automatically to save battery life, but if it's disabled you can turn it back on by:

1 Open **System Preferences**.

2 Select **Battery**.

3 Click **Automatic graphics switching**.

Turn off Location Services

A handful of apps and services use Location Services to see your current position. Siri, for example, can use your location to find nearby restaurants. You can save a small amount of battery life by turning Location Services off. To do this:

1 Open **System Preferences**, then select **Security & Privacy.**

2 Click the **Privacy** tab, then click the **padlock** icon.

3 Uncheck **Enable Location Services**.

Troubleshooting

What to do when something goes wrong...

Macs are incredibly reliable machines, and surprisingly free from viruses and hacking too, but even so, things can go wrong occasionally. That's because they're amongst the most complicated machines ever created, with miniaturised components that are nanometres in size, include dozens of sensors, and process millions of lines of software code. Throw in third-party apps, unpredictable environments, and physical damage, and something might go wrong.

If the worst does happen; such as a frozen screen, a crashing app, or a loss of battery life, then you don't always need to call the Genius Bar to get it fixed. Instead, there are a number of things you can try first to try and remedy the situation. Let's take a look at some of the things you can try when something goes wrong:

How to fix a frozen app

If an application freezes and won't close, macOS provides an easy way to force-quit it:

1 Click on the **Apple** logo in the menu bar, then choose **Force Quit**. If the menu has also frozen then you can try pressing **Command** > **Option** > **Escape** on the keyboard.

2 In the Force Quit window, look for the app which has crashed. It should say *(not responding)* in grey text. Select it then click the **Force Quit** button.

Use Disk Utility to scan for problems

If you suspect that something is wrong with your Mac's hard drive, then you can use Disk Utility to check for problems, and even fix them.

1 To find Disk Utility, open **Launchpad** from the Dock, click on the folder called **Other**, then click on **Disk Utility**.

2 Click on the drive you wish to check, then click **First Aid**. The app will then check for any problems with the drive, and if necessary fix them.

3 Try using the Recovery Drive app. To do this force your Mac to turn off by holding down the **Power** button, then turn it back on while holding down the **option** key. Select **Recovery HD**, then press **Enter** to boot it. If your Mac loads, use the Apple menu to restart it the normal way. Hopefully, everything will be okay this time.

Force your Mac to restart

If your Mac has become completely unresponsive, press and hold the **power** button for a few seconds and it will restart. If you're not sure, the power button is the small black square in the top-right corner of the keyboard.

Fix a Mac that won't turn on

If your Mac won't finish starting up, or won't boot at all, then there are some simple things you can try:

1. Make sure it's plugged in. This might sound silly, but if the power cable was unplugged or the wall switch was turned off, then your MacBook's battery might have drained without you knowing.

2. Try unplugging then replugging the power cord. Sometimes it becomes loose.

3. Try using the Recovery Drive app. To do this force your Mac to turn off by holding down the **Power** button, then turn it back on while holding down the **option** button. Select **Recovery HD**, then press **Enter** to boot it. If your Mac loads, use the Apple menu to restart it the normal way. Hopefully, everything will be okay this time.

4. If none of the above works, then it's time to call the Genius Bar at your local Apple Store and make an appointment to get your Mac looked at (see over the page for more details).

Reset the NVRAM

The NVRAM stores information about your Mac's screen resolution, speaker volume, startup disk and time. If you're having problems with any of these, then it's a good idea to reset the NVRAM. To do this:

1. Turn off your Mac. Turn it back on, and when you hear the startup chime press and hold the **Command** > **Option** > **P** > **R** keys.

2. If you've pressed the right keys, then your Mac will restart once more. You can now let go of the keys.

After your Mac finishes starting up, make sure to open System Preferences and adjust any settings that were reset, such as the sound volume, display resolution, startup disk, or time zone.

Locate or erase your Mac

Find your Mac using another computer or iOS device...

If the worst happens, and you lose your MacBook, first of all, don't panic! It might be somewhere obvious, like in another room, in a cupboard, or sitting on the table of a coffee shop (okay, that is a little worrying). If you've looked around and still can't find it, then here's how to track it down using iCloud, and even remotely erase its hard drive...

Use Find My iPhone to find your Mac

1. Use another device or computer and go to **www.icloud.com**.

2. Try to log in. If two-factor authentication is enabled and you're asked for a passcode, use your iPhone or iPad to get the code.

3. Once you're logged into iCloud, click the **Find iPhone** icon, then wait for your devices to load.

4. Click on your MacBook using the Map screen, or click the drop-down icon at the top of the screen and select it. In the pop-up panel you'll be able to play a sound, lock your Mac or erase it. See below for more details.

Erase your Mac

If the worst has happened and you don't think you'll be able to get your Mac back, then you can securely erase its contents to prevent someone from accessing your data. When erased an activation lock is enabled and Find My iPhone is automatically turned on. This means if if your Mac is ever restored by someone else you can still track it and be assured that they can't unlock it without your Apple ID and password.
After you've selected Erase:

- If it's online then your Mac will be immediately erased, and you'll get a confirmation email to let you know.
- If it's offline then it will be erased when it's next turned on. If you manage to find your Mac before it's turned on then you can cancel the erase by logging into iCloud, selecting your Mac then choosing Stop Erase Request.
- If it's erased and then you find it, you can restore the most recent backup from TimeMachine during the set-up process.

The Genius Bar

Get help when you need it most...

The Genius Bar is a technical support service in every Apple Store where you can get help to solve the problem or receive a replacement device.

They're often referred to as the heart and soul of an Apple Store. Every Genius Bar is manned by a team of technical specialists called "Geniuses". Each has experience solving every kind of hardware and software-related problems. They're also friendly and understanding to boot.

Most services at the Genius Bar are carried out for free. Repairs are carried out in the store, often while you wait, and if the Genius can't repair the device on the spot then a replacement is usually offered.

How to book a Genius Bar appointment

The easiest way to book a Genius Bar appointment is via the Apple Store website. The URL changes depending on your location, but Google search *"Book a Genius Bar appointment"* and the first result will take you to the right page. From the website you can select your nearest store and choose a suitable time and date – right down to the exact 10 minutes that suit your needs.

Keep in mind that the Genius Bar is a popular service, so the first available appointment might be weeks in advance.

Attending the Genius Bar

When you arrive at the Apple Store, check in with an employee holding a blue iPad. If you cant see them through the crowd, look for any other employee in a blue shirt, they'll be able to help. Alternatively, you can check in using the Apple Store app, but being met face-to-face is always more reassuring.

Once you're at the Genius Bar be polite and explain the problem with your device. The Genius team help dozens of customers each day, so it's likely they've encountered every kind of problem and should be able to quickly identify what's wrong with your device. From there, follow their advice, and hopefully you'll have a working Mac once again within a short period of time.

Index

Stay inspired

Other Ultimate Guides:

iPad:
Ultimate Guide

978-1-914347-07-8

$19.75 USA

$22.99 CAN

£10.99 UK

$22.99 AUD

iPhone 13:
Ultimate Guide

978-1-914347-96-2

$19.75 USA

$22.99 CAN

£10.99 UK

$22.99 AUD

iPad Pro:
Ultimate Guide

978-1-914347-05-4

$19.75 USA

$22.99 CAN

£10.99 UK

$22.99 AUD

iPhone:
Ultimate Guide

978-1-914347-06-1

$19.75 USA

$22.99 CAN

£10.99 UK

$22.99 AUD

Tesla:
Ultimate Guide

978-1-914347-04-7

$19.75 USA

$22.99 CAN

£10.99 UK

$22.99 AUD

Seniors Guides: Other Guides:

Seniors Guide to
iPad

978-1-914347-01-6

$19.75 USA

$22.99 CAN

£10.99 UK

$22.99 AUD

Seniors Guide to
MacBook

978-1-914347-02-3

$19.75 USA

$22.99 CAN

£10.99 UK

$22.99 AUD

Seniors Guide to
iPhone

978-1-914347-00-9

$19.75 USA

$22.99 CAN

£10.99 UK

$22.99 AUD

iMac Guide

979-8699016419

$12.98 USA

$14.98 CAN

£9.98 UK

Alexa: Complete
Guide

978-1-914347-03-0

$19.75 USA

$22.99 CAN

£10.99 UK

$22.99 AUD

Visit www.leafpublishing.co.uk to find out more

Manufactured by Amazon.ca
Bolton, ON

25296623R00090